# The New
# Digital
# Video
# Manual

THIS IS A CARLTON BOOK

Text and design copyright © 2002, 2008 Carlton Books Limited
Pictures © Various (see page 160)

This edition published in 2008 by Carlton Books Ltd
A division of the Carlton Publishing Group
20 Mortimer Street
London
W1T 3JW

A CIP catalogue for this book is available from the British Library

ISBN: 978 1 84732 045 2

Executive Editors: Sarah Larter, Gareth Jones
Editorial: Chris Hawkes, David Ballheimer, Ahren Warner
Design: Tyrone Taylor, Mike Spender
Senior Art Editor: Gülen Shevki-Taylor
Picture Research: Lorna Ainger, Steve Behan
Production: Lisa Moore

Printed in Dubai

# The New Digital Video Manual

An essential, up-to-date guide
to the equipment, skills and
techniques of digital videomaking

## Robert Hull, Jamie Ewbank & Christian Darkin

**CARLTON**
BOOKS

# :::CONTENTS:::::::::::::::::::::::::::::::::

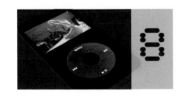

# INTRODUCTION

Videomaking should always be an adventure, you are an experienced producer of your own movies or whether you just press the big red record button on special occasions. Every time you put the viewfinder to your eye, or gaze at the LCD screen on your camcorder, you are about to embark on a marvelous journey, which, even with the best planning, will take you to places and put you in situations you might perhaps only have dreamed about.

We hope that by the end of this book you will be prepared to make even more journeys into the unknown with your camcorder, because seeing what you have recorded, in any capacity – whether it be at home on your TV, on the internet, or even in competition with other videos – will give you an enormous buzz. Even experienced videomakers still get goosebumps when they see an amazing shot or a sequence they have created. It might have come by chance, it might have taken an age to plan and shoot, but, whatever it is, it is the outcome that matters. And you will soon discover, if you talk to anyone involved in film or videomaking, that these are the moments they live for.

With the best will in the world, reading a book is not going to make you a videomaker; however, having the basics locked away somewhere in the little grey cells can be a godsend. So, with that in mind, we set to the task of developing this book. Ultimately, we decided that the basics, quite frankly, were not going to be enough (and it would make this a pamphlet, not a book!). Instead, we thought it best to give you a taste of the whole shooting match, from the basics to the downright complicated – and yes, we thought it only right to include computer jargon as well!

The growth of digital technology has been enormous. Now, as we continue to edge into the twenty-first century, the range of equipment and its capabilities – available to videomakers with all sorts of budgets – is bewildering. Not only is it possible to pick up a high-quality camcorder for a reasonable price but, with the advent of computer-based, non-linear editing, it is no exaggeration to state that professional-quality editing is possible from the PC in the living room or bedroom. The hours of faffing around with an edit VCR have now been replaced by the hours of faffing around with a PC or Mac!

It is also important to remember that even within the digital realm, technology is changing. The internet is exploding as a medium for digital video and camcorders are popping up in all kinds of devices from phones to MP3 players. In just the same way that people use a word processor even if they don't consider themselves writers, everybody now is shooting video, even if they don't consider themselves as filmmakers.

Watch the news and you'll see video from mobile phones alongside video shot by professional journalists. Contact a family member abroad and the chances are you'll be able to see them on webcam. Watch a presentation at the office and it may well contain video clips. Visit YouTube and you'll pretty soon convince yourself that everything everyone ever does is being recorded and put online. Video is the new medium of communication – not just from broadcasters to us, but from everyone to everyone. It's now not just our entertainment, it's our social interaction. It's not just a way of telling stories, but a part of those stories. And that trend can only grow.

Amid all this exciting new technology one point shines out like a beacon: no matter what technology you use, you are only as good as the shots you take and the cuts you make. In the future, being literate with video is likely to become as important as being literate with words. And so, with that, we suggest that you read on...

**ROBERT HULL, JAMIE EWBANK
AND CHRISTIAN DARKIN**

GETTING

# GETTING STARTED

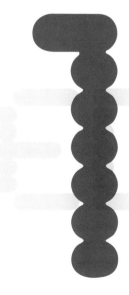

# GETTING STARTED

GETTING STARTED

**A**lthough digital technology is undoubtedly the future of video-making, it is worth knowing a little about the camcorder's past.

### A BRIEF HISTORY OF CAMCORDERS

According to myth and legend — well actually according to Sony — the first consumer camcorder was launched way back in 1980. However it wasn't until 1985 that a real battleground emerged with Sony launching the 8mm recording format, while JVC introduced its compact version of the VHS format, in VHS-C.

Consumers now had access to machines which were both a camera and a recorder, hence **cam**era and re**corder,** whereas previously they had been seen wandering around with two separate boxes, one for taking the images, the other for recording them.

### Early Days

These first machines used analogue recording methods and as such the quality of the pictures was somewhat below that seen on a television screen. The United Kingdom, Australia, New Zealand and parts of Western Europe use the **PAL** (Phase Alternating Line) TV colour standard, which builds a television picture through 625 horizontal lines. France

uses the **Secam** standard (again 625 lines), while the USA and Japan use the **NTSC** standard (525 horizontal lines). While not all these lines are used for creating the images — some are simply used for providing information — the fact that both the 8mm and VHS-C formats were capable of a line resolution of around 240 lines gives you some indication as to the picture quality on offer.

However, despite the somewhat duff picture quality, camcorders became a desirable product throughout the late 1980s and early 1990s as household after household fell for the novelty value of seeing yourself

*Fig 1 – Home video-making has been a popular hobby for decades but it took the advent of camcorders to bring it to the masses.*

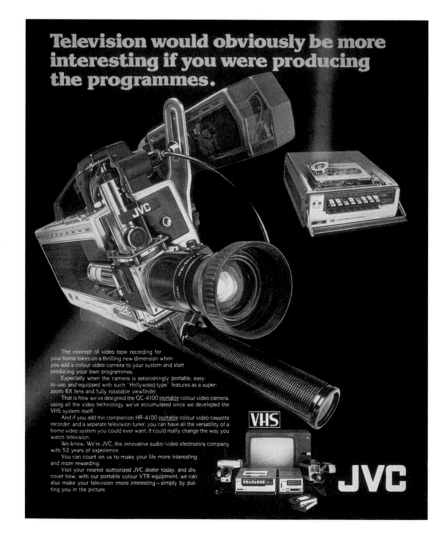

*Fig 2–4 – Analogue camcorders like these have now been replaced by superior digital models.*

and your friends on video. Camcorder sales peaked in the early 1990s due to the success of manufacturers providing smaller camcorders with increased features, at more affordable prices. It has also helped that some of the most popular television programmes worldwide (such as Britain's *You've Been Framed* and *America's Funniest Home Videos)* are devoted to home movies.

## A New Breed

Every dog has its day, however, and though still popular in the mid-1990s, the camcorder's moment in the spotlight was ebbing away. The arrival of new technology: home cinema, DVD, mobile phones, gaming technology and the internet, meant consumers' attention was divided even further, and consequently video-making lost out.

Fortunately, the major electronics manufacturers had a trick up their sleeves that would make videomaking vital again. In 1995 Sony produced the world's first digital camcorder, the DCR-VX1000. This large, not especially attractive, camcorder recorded onto small digital cassettes using the Mini DV (Digital Video) format. Images were crisp, clear and full of detail, the camcorder had several important manual controls and high-quality digital sound. It was also possible to add an external microphone.

Although hardly aimed at the general or casual user, it provided a tantalizing taster of what was to come. The term "Broadcast Quality" – often the barometer of whether footage was good enough to be shown on television or the cinema screen – was about to take a battering. Context became the important issue.

Quick to spot the benefits of the VX1000 the BBC soon bought a plentiful supply. To its cameramen and women, used to lugging around larger format film and

*Fig 5 – Sony's DCR-VX1000, the world's first digital camcorder.*

video cameras, the VX1000 was not a large camera. In fact it allowed them to take camcorders into previously undiscovered areas. The era of the fly-on-the-wall, "docusoap" and reality TV show was upon us.

## Bigger is Not Always Better

Following the launch of the VX1000, JVC, Panasonic and Canon soon followed with their own DV models and a contest of miniaturization began. Every quarter, as launches were made, there would be a new claim for the world's smallest camcorder. The range of designs on the market became bewildering: you could have an upright or "book"-style DV camcorder, a rectangular-styled palmcorder, a camcorder that looked like an SLR camera, or, if simplicity was your bag, a square camcorder.

As the list of digital camcorders grew towards the end of the 1990s, so did the amount of features available to the consumer. Digital effects and zooms increased, video lights were added, batteries were made smaller, LCD screens were made bigger. Soon it became possible to take digital snaps with your camcorder and decide whether you wanted to store them on tape or on a supplied storage card. You could, therefore, have the best of both worlds – a way of taking both moving and still images. Yet, despite this rush, some seasoned videomakers felt the new camcorders were selling them short.

In the early days, camcorder controls were large and easy to operate, and control over focus, exposure, zoom, white balance and shutter speeds was manual. With the increasing miniaturization, these features were being sacrificed for functions that made it easier for a salesmen to "sell" the camcorder. A camcorder with a 500x-digital zoom is virtually unusable, as the camcorder needs to be completely steady, or either the shot will be lost or the amount of **pixellation** (distortion) of the image will be so high as to make the image unintelligible.

## Something For Everyone

To this end the camcorder market now divides into three distinct sections: budget, entry-level and enthusiast. There are consumer camcorders available for both under £100 and over £3,000, and at many price points in between. What is more, the level of design is now sophisticated enough to be able to distinguish between the different needs of the variety of customers. Enthusiast camcorders have more manual control over sound and video, have less digital and picture effects – in general, less gimmicks. They tend to be slightly larger and more complicated to use than their counterparts in the budget and entry-level sectors. Here you will find a real dogfight for your money. Feature counts will be

*Fig 6 – Small is beautiful: modern camcorders are light and portable.*

high, but corners might have been cut in terms of build quality, as well as image and sound quality.

Right at the bottom end of the market, you can pick up a camcorder recording onto memory cards for just a few tens of pounds and because these machines have no moving parts, they are both tiny and very tough.

In addition, the world of camcorders is being rapidly encroached upon by devices which would never have been considered as videocameras in the past. Stills cameras, mobile phones and mp3 players are now capable of recording video and these have become ubiquitous to the point at which when a major news event occurs, it would be unusual *not* to see eyewitness pictures from the scene, courtesy of some bystander's phone.

However, as video-making continues its dash into the twenty-first century, the range of products on offer to consumers has never been greater, nor has the range of quality of camcorders been higher. With digital videomaking now more affordable, and editing and distribution more instantly available to all, there is now virtually no limit on what can be achieved, whether it be from the comfort of your living room, or as part of a semi-professional set-up. Digital video-making now dovetails beautifully with the power of desktop video. Computers and camcorders can now meet and, within a few hours, videos can be stitched together with basic cuts and transitions, or, for the more ambitious, with hitherto very expensive special effects.

### Changing the Old Order

Even film-makers have had to take note of the power of digital video, as traditionalists used to cutting on film have made way for the power of the pixel and the PC. Hollywood is increasingly utilizing the flexibility and time-saving aspects of digital video. Initially, this was in the post-production houses famous for adding the "special" bit to film effects, but now this now routinely includes shooting feature films on digital video cameras.

Camcorders can now record onto tapes, DVDs, hard disks or memory cards. You can even plug your laptop into your HD camcorder and take footage straight to the computer – cutting out the camcorder's media altogether.

*Fig 7 – The Canon XL H1 – a definite enthusiast's camcorder.*

It is easy to be blinded by the speed of technology, but through this tremendously accelerated journey it is worth bearing in mind that, ultimately, while technology will help you make your ideas a reality, you have got to be able to point the camera in the right direction and know which button to press before you can do it. You can't put a price on basic video-making know-how!

### Sound

Audio has always been something of a troubling matter for camcorders. The microphones included on all but the most expensive (and high end) camcorders are generally one of the cheapest components used. Consequently sound quality does not always match the clarity of the images recorded. Even with digital technology there is a disparity between the quality of the images and audio. As a rule, most camcorders use **PCM** (Pulse Code Modulation) stereo sound. This is audio that has been digitized. It is available in two settings: 16-bit (48kHz, two channels) and 12-bit (32kHz, two from four channels). The first setting provides the highest-quality sound recording, often claimed to be slightly better than CD quality, though in reality slightly worse! The second setting does not produce as dynamic or fully rounded a sound, but as it only records onto two, out of four, channels, a further two channels are left open for adding narration or soundtrack dialogue/music at a later date.

**From Analogue to Digital: A Camcorder Timeline**

• *1980:* Sony introduces first consumer camcorder in Japan.

• *1985:* Sony launches 8mm recording format. JVC counters with the introduction of the VHS-C format, a compact version of its VHS technology.

• *1988:* JVC ups the ante with arrival of Super VHS (S-VHS) format.

• *1989:* Touché! Sony reacts with the Hi8 format, offering videomakers increased picture quality, and eventually stereo sound.

• *1995:* First Mini DV (Digital Video) camcorder arrives in the UK. It is the Sony DCR-VX1000, and though it costs significantly more than analogue consumer camcorders it is soon adopted by TV companies, production companies and semi-professional videomakers due to its exceptional picture quality.

• *1996* JVC and Panasonic launch DV camcorders into the UK market. JVC's GR-DV1 is the first example of a palmcorder, so called because it is so small it fits neatly into the user's hand.

• *1997* An omen of things to come? DVD players having been on sale in Japan for a year, are now available in the USA. Hitachi tries to change the camcorder market, unveiling its MP-EG1A camcorder towards the end of the year. This is the first tapeless camcorder, using MPEG compression to record digital images onto an internal hard disk. Image quality is unimpressive and price seems too high for consumers – it flops.

• *1999:* Sony introduces the Digital8 format. These new camcorders allow the user to record digital images onto analogue 8mm/Hi8 tape. Backwards compatibility means you can replay your existing 8mm/Hi8 tapes in the new machines!

• *2000:* Hitachi and Sony announce plans for new camcorders. Hitachi's plans include a DVD camcorder, while Sony unleashes a MiniDisc camcorder.

• *2001:* Hitachi's DZ-MV100 DVD RAM camcorder goes on sale for around f 1,800. Sony hits back, however, with a brand-new format MICROMV. Recording onto tapes smaller than Mini DV cassettes and using MPEG2 compression. The tapes are doomed, but the compression stays.

*Fig 8 – The JVC HD7.*

• *2002:* Camcorders start to appear on mobile phones. Camcorder technology is now so small, cheap and light that it can be included in a whole range of pocket devices.

• *2004:* Sony launches the HDR-FX1 – the world's first High Definition consumer camcorder, producing images of far higher quality than those being transmitted on television.

• *2005:* YouTube launched, allowing users across the world to view and share video clips. For the first time, anyone can put video online.

• *2007:* Blu-ray becomes available – the first technology allowing HD video to be recorded onto disk, although HDTVs and players are still quite rare.

In reality, the audio performance of most camcorders is acceptable rather than inspiring, and generally when you start looking at small machines, memory card camcorders and non-camcorder devices, the quality drops significantly.

### Non-Linear Editing

Aside from the improved performance criteria, digital camcorders have also helped support the growth in computer-based editing. This is commonly known as non-linear editing (NLE), as footage can be chopped, changed and moved around at will, rather than being edited in a linear fashion. Computer hardware and software is necessary for this although all PCs and Macs now come with basic editing tools built into their operating systems and more advanced editors can be purchased quite cheaply, and footage is often displayed on the computer monitor in a form known as a "timeline". This shows video and audio information which can then be re-ordered and have titles, transitions and effects added to it.

All tape based camcorders incorporate a **Firewire** socket among their terminals. This is a connection protocol developed by Sony, which allows for data communication at very high transfer rates. It can often be referred to by its technical name, IEEE-1394, but is more commonly known as Firewire.

Generally, footage can be transferred from a camcorder to either a PC or a Mac through a Firewire cable or a USB port. Once on disk, provided you have the right hardware and software, you can run amok with your footage, adding bits, trimming clips, changing the running order — as well as at a later date creating your own Video CDs, internet movies or DVDs.

### Facing the Future

And what about the future? Well, with analogue camcorders now extinct, the future is digital. That much is clear. It's pretty certain that the future is High Definition, although it will be a while before that's a standard on your mobile phone.

*Fig 9 – Nowadays, anything with a lens can record video – including mobile phones and stills cameras.*

In the medium term the idea that video is recorded onto a physical medium using lots of delicate moving parts (be it tape or DVD) and then played back to record the data onto your computer will take a serious knocking from systems which are faster, more flexible and less breakable.

Compression and storage space will be the key – right now, the problem with all digital formats is that the picture and sound have to be compressed to give you a decent amount of filming time. That limits both the resolution of the images and their clarity, but compression is just software, and it will get better even as storage space increases.

In the longer term, video machines will be shaped by what they're used for, and with video rapidly becoming a medium of communication for all on the internet and in everyday life, it's likely that working with video will become as natural and easy as working with words – with sending a video message as routine as making a phonecall, or writing an email.

After all, a camcorder is just a lens and a microphone. Everything else – the resolution of the images, the editing, the way the signal is stored, combined or transmitted – can, and will, be up to you.

### BUYING THE RIGHT DIGITAL CAMCORDER

The most common question asked of anyone "in the know" about camcorders is usually, which one should I buy? It is not that it is an impossible question to answer, it is just that once consumers realize the

potential number of answers, their buying decision seems to become more complicated.

Cost is the most important consideration when buying a camcorder. The range of camcorders on offer is huge, and because of canny marketing there is a model that will appeal to everyone, but consumers need to know how much they can spend, in order that they can be advised properly. As we mentioned previously, the camcorder market is divided into three sections: budget, entry-level and enthusiast. Obviously prices change rapidly and there is no way of keeping track of them during the lifetime of a book, so you should keep your eyes trained on the videomaking press and price comparison sites on the internet. However, as a rough guide, the three sections break down this way:

*Budget:* Prices generally sub £100 to around £300
*Entry-level:* Prices generally £300 to around £800.
*Enthusiast:* Price generally £800 to about £6,000

What you get for your money is vastly different. Enthusiast camcorders are usually larger than their counterparts, have a wide selection of manual controls, have advanced level of socketry including

*Fig 10 – One of the most popular uses for camcorders is to create lasting memories of idyllic holidays.*

Firewire in and out, analogue inputs and outputs, and will require an investment of your time to learn how to use them effectively. Camcorders in the other two sections will mix and match features and functions, with an increasing number of digital and picture effects becoming available, while manual features – the favourites of any experienced videomaker as it allows them to control how the footage is recorded – will take a back seat. Budget camcorders are designed to be very easy to use, and to provide reasonable results "for the money", but they won't have the flexibility or control of more expensive models.

Once you have decided on what user you want to be your choice becomes a lot easier. If all that you want is an easy-to-use camcorder for recording the odd family event, then there is absolutely no point in shelling out £1,500 on a model with all the features that a semi-pro would want. And likewise, if you want to shoot a feature film you will be left wanting if you are tempted by the sub-£100-price of a memory card model.

## DIGITAL FORMATS

In order to buy the right camcorder you should first decide on the right format. There are currently several important formats on the market and more appear all the time.

### Mini DVD

Tapes are smaller than a box of matches, affordable and capable of producing images and audio at a quality still transmitted by most TV channels. Tape lengths vary but are available in 30, 60- and 90-minute options. Footage is imported into a computer via a firewire socket and eats hard disk space at 3.6MB per second.

### HDV

High Definition DVD camcorders use standard DV tapes, but compress their footage in a completely different way to allow full HD footage to be recorded. Images are superior to anything else on the market offering 1080 or 720 lines of resolution, although you'll need a HD TV or a computer to see the benefit.

### DVD-RAM

The camcorder records digital images, sound and stills, using MPEG2 compression, onto an 8cm rewritable

*Fig 11 – Camcorders are getting smaller and far easier to take with you ... anywhere.*

DVD disk, housed in a caddy that fits into the left-hand side of the camcorder. Most home DVD players will play most camcorder DVDs, but it's not a guarantee, so check your models before you buy. You can select the quality at which your footage is compressed, but the highest quality only gets you about 18 minutes of footage on a disk and even then it's not quite up to the standard of DV (almost but not quite).

### HDD

First developed by JVC, HDD machines record onto their own internal hard disk drive just like that on your computer. You don't need to worry about tapes and the machine can record tens of hours of footage before it needs to be transferred to a computer and wiped, so it's great for a long trip. HDD machines are compact and the quality of their recording depends entirely on the compression used, so in theory, they could surpass any other format. In practice, you'll need to check the model you plan to buy carefully. Don't just look through the viewfinder – get hold of full quality footage and examine it close-up on a big screen.

### CARD MEMORY

Card memory camcorders record onto the same memory card media that stills cameras use. They're tiny and have no moving parts, so they're extremely robust and won't even flicker if you tape them to your clothing during extreme sports. They're also dirt cheap – you can pick up a new one on eBay for £20. However, watch out for both recording quality and resolution. Many machines compress their video very highly and some record at as low as 640x480 resolution or less (enough for the internet, but nothing much else). Good ones are more expensive, but can rival HD machines (although memory card space is key if you record high quality images).

### FIREWIRE (DV-IN-AND-OUT)

Firewire sockets allow the DV signal to transfer between suitably equipped devices, the most common cases being a digital camcorder and a computer. All digital camcorders have a Firewire socket, but only a small percentage of them allow the digital signal to be sent and received. Hence you will see plenty of camcorders referred to as DV-out, but few as DV-in-and-out.

DV-out only means you can transfer your DV footage to the computer for editing, but once there you cannot transfer it back to a blank DV tape waiting in your camcorder.

The reason for the lack of DV-in-and-out camcorders has long been a moot point. Manufacturers claim that in the eyes of Customs and Excise a DV camcorder capable of recording a signal from another source is also a VCR (Video Cassette Recorder) and liable to more duty. Therefore, the price of a DV-in-and-out model is usually more than that of a DV-out only. In their wisdom, camcorder manufacturers took it upon themselves to claim that consumers would not be willing to pay the extra for DV-in-and-out. Nowadays, hard disk space is so cheap that many videomakers choose to archive their work not to tape but to a spare hard drive: this diminishes the need for DV inputs.

Non-tape machines usually transfer using a USB connection. Typically this makes your camcorder appear as an extra drive on your computer from which footage can be copied. The only thing you generally have to worry about is whether the compression system used by your camcorder is editable and playable with your computer's software.

### ANALOGUE INPUTS

Generally found on enthusiast models, analogue

*Figs 12–13 – Camcorders can be used as digital stills cameras and have removable storage media.*

*Fig 14 – Socketry is an important factor in selecting a camcorder.*

inputs allow an analogue source i.e. an old camcorder or VCR to be connected to the digital camcorder. It is then possible to record the analogue material onto digital tape – and from there transfer it to your computer. This is a useful way of archiving material in a digital format, and giving new life to material shot in the pre-digital era or on analogue camcorders.

*Fig 15 – Sock-et to 'em: Analogue, Firewire and PC connections.*

## MANUAL CONTROLS

A must if you want to take videomaking seriously and take control of your productions. All but the most basic DV camcorders will allow you to take manual control over focus, but you will have to check specifications carefully if you want manual exposure, shutter speeds, iris or white balance controls.

On enthusiast models the manual controls tend to involve larger buttons, and potentially a manual focus ring around the lens, rather than a small thumbwheel on the side or back of the camcorder. Don't just check that your machine has manual controls – check how they're operated. A manual focus ring or touch-screen is far more convenient than trying to focus using buttons.

### Zoom

It's an easy adage to remember: optical zoom = good, digital zoom = bad!

One of the easiest videomaking mistakes to make is to overuse the zoom. Check out your favourite films and television shows and see how little the professionals use it, and when they do, why it is often purely stylistic. If you want to see something closer, move closer to it!

Optical zooms can run up to 25x magnification, a perfectly adequate number, which creates no picture degradation. Digital zooms can run up to 700x magnification and increase pixellation (picture noise) on your images, while also causing you to use a tripod in order to keep the camcorder steady enough to see anything. If you are still interested in digital zoom perhaps it is worth asking yourself: is the best way to record your favourite image by standing ten miles away from it?

### Image Stabilization

Two image stabilization systems have grown up over the years. Optical and Digital (Electronic). Video purists have often hankered solely after the optical system, as it does not electronically alter the image in order to keep it steady, and therefore your footage will not suffer from any picture noise. However, optical systems increase the size of a camcorder and in the age of miniaturization, the digital system has become more prevalent. This system, sensing camcorder shake, electronically enlarges a 70 per cent portion of your image and stores this to tape instead. The camcorder then compares each image with the last and moves this enlarged portion up and down in order to keep the key elements in the same position.

Initially digital stabilization was prone to the problem of increasing picture noise, but recent systems have shown a marked improvement.

However, the best form of image stabilization known to videomakers is still a tripod!

### SOCKETS

Small things, but things that are often overlooked, the inclusion of key sockets on your camcorder can often make the difference between a polished production and a gremlin-encrusted nightmare. The two most important, after DV-in-and-out or USB, are an external microphone socket and a headphone jack. The first allows you to bypass the basic microphone on your camcorder and invest in a far more subtle and sophisticated version, which is likely to give you a fuller, more directional sound.

The headphone jack is important for enabling you to hear what your camcorder is recording in the audio department. This is useful for picking up fluffed lines, over-flying aircraft, squeaks, buzzes and other noises you might not necessarily want on your footage.

### VIEWFINDER/LCD

Digital camcorders invariably feature both optical viewfinders and LCD screens. They can both be used for framing images, but the LCD screen does place extra draw on the camcorder battery. LCD screens range in size from around 4.5 centimetres (1.8 inches) to 9 centimetres (3.5 inches) and are always colour. They are best used for reviewing footage, and as most camcorders have built-in speakers, you can watch and listen to footage taken only seconds ago. The larger the LCD screen the more money you will pay, but be warned: LCD screens hate bright sunlight, and can often be rendered useless by it.

Viewfinders are now predominantly colour, though traditionalists have always preferred black-and-white viewfinders for the exposure and contrast "hints" they give. Sadly, even high-end, enthusiast camcorders now use colour view-finders, though you can find accessories for some of these camcorders, such as Canon's DM-XL1 or DM-XL1 S, which include black-and-white viewfinders.

Again miniaturization has caused viewfinders to be reduced in size, so, if only from a comfort point of view, be sure to check the eyepiece you might be gazing down for hours on end is comfortable.

### AUDIO

If you want flexibility in the audio department, look out for camcorders which feature audio dub – most camcorders utilizing 16-bit and 12-bit PCM stereo sound feature it, but not all. Audio mix is also another useful function, as it allows you to balance the level of sound coming from the different stereo channels.

*Fig 16 – An optical zoom of up to 25x magnification is more than adequate for most video-making.*

*Fig 17 – LCD screens are useful for reviewing footage that you have just shot.*

## DIGITAL STILLS STORAGE

Do you want your camcorder to be your camera as well? If so, virtually every camcorder from budget models to enthusiast camcorders can oblige. Previously restricted to storing snaps to Mini DV tape, digital camcorders now record high-quality stills to multimedia cards. Images can be printed out via computer or sent as email attachments. The number of still images that can be stored depends on the MegaByte (MB) capacity of the storage card. Image quality has improved to a point where some enthusiast camcorders are capable of stills approaching the quality of 35mm film.

## CHOOSING THE RIGHT COMPUTER

Let's start by saying they're all okay. Any recently purchased computer should be up to the task of video editing. That said, "up to the task" doesn't mean optimal and you need to keep your machine free from clutter (like spyware, viruses, constantly running programs and bits of your old video projects) and running at its best (i.e defragment your hard drives regularly) to keep your editing a smooth and enjoyable experience.

Even laptops are okay for video editing as long as you've got the hard drive space and many small scale video projects are done on-location using just a camcorder and a laptop.

## HD and SD

High definition work places more demands on your computer than DV. Think about it – your machine is having to deal with four times as many pixels in every frame and so when you start adding effects, fades, mixes, titles, colour correction and multiple layers of video and audio, things can start to slow down.

Smaller video formats can also place extra demands on your system. The tools for compressing video used by state-of-the-art camcorders are designed to use all the computer's power to make the video as compact as possible so you can put more on a disk, drive or memory card. That means your computer has to work hard to unpack each frame of that video as you're editing it.

## Power and memory

The processor is what's going to be doing the tough work of decoding your video, working out which bits to play back from which files and what effects need to be applied to them, rendering the effects, and doing all the donkey work of editing video. Most processors can do this standing on their heads, but the key issue is speed. The more effects, video and audio layers, different types of video, colour correction filters, transitions, etc. that you pile onto your timeline, the slower, jerkier and more pixellated playback is going to be. Your finished movie will still be rendered at full quality, but if you can't accurately see what's going on as you edit, you can't make the best editing decisions.

The computer's internal memory also has an effect on the smoothness of your editing experience. Generally, get as much memory as you can afford because that's what stops the system from juddering to a halt during playback. It also

*Fig 18 – Modern computers all have the ability to edit video built in.*

## Compression and Disk Space

You can never have enough disk space for video. DV and HDV both take up 3.6MB per second. That means an hour of video takes up 12.96GB, but that's not the end of the story. Want to make a wedding video? Well, say that's 1.5 hours of finished programme, but you'll also need to capture probably have 5 hours of footage before you can start editing. You'll also need 5GB of room left to prepare your finished DVD. That's nearly 100GB for a modest project.

If your project is more adventurous, you might also need space for title animations, different versions of the project and effects (which are usually rendered with *no* compression – i.e. up to 2MB per *frame* – or 50MB per second).

As if that wasn't enough, to get the best performance out of your editor, it's good practice to store the video footage, audio footage and editing software on completely separate hard drives. This means that the guts of the drive aren't having to continually search back and forth as the computer switches between different tasks.

The good news is that hard drives are cheap and although a regular video editor might end up with a lot of them (I'm looking at five hooked up to the machine I'm typing on right now). They're relatively inexpensive and you can buy external USB or Firewire drives, which you can plug in or take out at will.

*Fig 19 – Most video hardware will plug into a USB or Firewire port.*

gives your computer a kind of internal sketch pad on which it can keep frames of video, rendered effects and other items it might need instant access to as you work. This process will be invisible to you, but it will keep things running fast and smoothly.

Increasingly, software is taking the responsibility for drawing your effects away from your main processor and giving it to your graphics card. This frees up the processor to think about other things, but means that although the final look of your video and the time it takes to render that finished programme doesn't have anything to do with the power of your graphics card, the smoothness of the playback you'll get while editing is more and more dependent on it. And smooth playback during editing is what makes the difference between enjoying the process and hating it.

A good rule of thumb is that if you play modern videogames on your computer, the chances are you've got a good video card.

*Fig 20 – When it comes to PCs, Dell have a well-deserved reputation for quality.*

## Mac and PC

Neither the Mac nor the PC has the edge on video editing. They're both fine systems which are well tuned to video work and which companies are putting a lot of effort into designing video software for.

There's more of it for the PC, so you've got more choice and because of that, there's more competition which means that new innovations spread faster through the marketplace and software has to be well written and competitively priced to succeed. That said, the Mac is famously easy to work with. It doesn't bother you with the finer details of what it's doing with your files and doesn't bang on constantly about how much work it's having to do on your behalf.

## Software

Software is probably the most important consideration when setting up a computer for video work. Both the PC and the Mac come with basic video editing tools (Windows Movie Maker in the case of the PC and iMovies in the case of the Mac). IMovie has the edge, and you can put together a basic movie with either. However neither of them are particularly powerful products and most users will probably want to graduate quite quickly to a more comprehensive piece of software.

On the PC side, this means one of the huge range of budget editing packages on the market. There are too many to list here, but some of the most popular are:

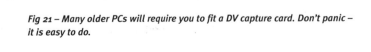

*Fig 21 – Many older PCs will require you to fit a DV capture card. Don't panic – it is easy to do.*

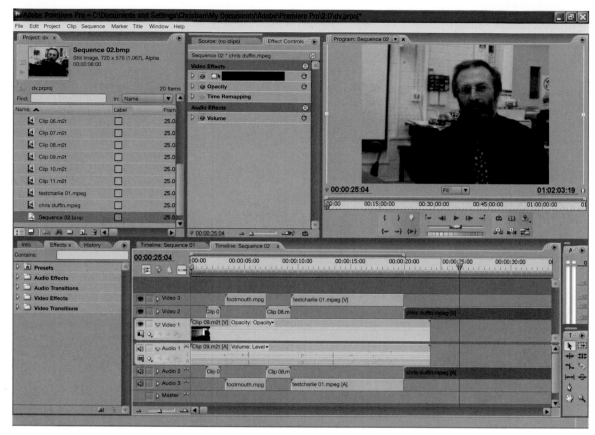

*Fig 22 – Modern editing software contains everything you need to produce professional videos.*

*Videowave:* An editor which concentrates on ease of use, but sometimes sacrifices features.

*Premiere Elements:* Probably the most versatile of the budget editors, Elements takes a while to learn but includes many high-end tools.

*Pinnacle Studio:* Easy to use and powerful. This editor does have limitations, but its one-button solutions to common problems are welcome.

*Ulead Video Studio:* Aother simple but powerful editing package which allows you to produce good results fast.

On the Mac side, *Final Cut Express HD* is the frontrunner. This is a cut-down version of their professional editing software, so you'll be able to graduate to *Final Cut Pro* without re-learning all your techniques.

These packages all offer DV and HD editing, and although the range of features varies considerably, they will all allow you to produce some fairly impressive results at up to about £100. If you want to go further and do sophisticated edits (L-cuts and J-cuts – see Chapter 6 (pages 108–129) and layered keyframed effects, as well as working with complex sound sequences and multiple layers of video, you'll need to spend a little more and move towards packages like *Premiere Pro* on the PC or *Final Cut Pro* on the Mac. These are professional tools that you'll need to work hard to get the best from, but they'll allow you to produce work up to the standard of the best in television and film (as long as you have the skill and the shot material!).

## BUYING THE RIGHT ACCESSORIES

To capture the best images and audio you need more than just a camcorder, you need accessories! Chosen and used wisely these can help to add professional touches to your videos and they also help to make you a more proficient and organized producer. The

*Fig 23* – **The Shining,** *directed by Stanley Kubrick, used the innovative Steadicam system.*

*Fig 24 – Get yourself some support! A tripod is a videomaking necessity.*

miniaturization of technology attendant to digital video has seen many videomakers discard what are otherwise essential tools. Never assume that the tiny dimensions of your camcorder, and the quality of digital video don't need a helping hand from time to time. There's a wide array of accessories on offer, and though you don't necessarily need to possess all of them, it will be beneficial to have a selection.

## Camcorder Supports

A tripod is the most important accessory you can have. It will enable you to shoot from a wide variety of angles and heights, and from a stable platform, and for these reasons it is essential. Prices range from very cheap to staggeringly expensive. Tripods aimed at semi-professional and professional users are incredibly stable, but weigh a prodigious amount. Depending on the cost of the tripod these set-ups can be sold separately, so you purchase a video head and a set of tripod legs that you then combine. Remember in professional productions there's always someone to cart the gear around, whereas in your productions it could well just be you!

If you are going to be shooting regularly you will need a durable tripod that offers aluminium and/or graphite construction, a spirit level – either on the tripod head or legs – to ensure your shots are even, and a quick-release platform. This allows you to slide the camcorder on and off the tripod without having to unscrew the bolt that attaches the camcorder to the quick release platform. This is most beneficial when you are moving around a location and setting up new shots.

There are other forms of camcorder support, such as a monopod, which is a single leg version of the tripod. Naturally it does not provide as much stability but is useful in locations where space is at a premium. It is also lighter, and invariably cheaper than a tripod. A chest pod can also be used to brace the camcorder against you for stability. Finally it's also worth mentioning Steadicam systems.

Created during the making of Stanley Kubrick's *The Shining,* Steadicam is a support that has no contact with the floor. Instead it uses a system of weights and counterweights below the camcorder to keep it level. It allows the camcorder operator to move freely with the camcorder and shoot smooth footage, as well as allowing you to get closer to the action. Professional systems are prohibitively expensive for most amateur productions but there are cut-down, budget systems available which offer many of the same benefits.

*Fig 25 – Cover star. Your camcorder is precious so keep it protected from the elements.*

## Camcorder Protectors

Received wisdom says you don't get your camcorder wet – as it will not work! However, there are occasions where you might be shooting footage around, near or even in water, and, yep, it can also start raining. So, what can you do? Inexpensive rainjackets are available to cover the camcorder in light rain, and more substantial protection is on offer from some of the accessory companies in the back of this book. Underwater housing for many DV camcorders is also available. A number of manufacturers can tailor-make a housing for you, but both camcorder makers and accessory firms supply one-size-fits-all options.

*Fig 26 – Using filters opens you up to some intriguing effects.*

*Figs 27–28 – Lens converters are a useful way of adding depth and drama to your videos, but the same effects can be achieved using post-production software.*

## Filters

A filter is a piece of material that is placed in front of the camcorder lens in order to modify the light entering it, and it can be used for special effects.

The range of filters on offer is incredibly diverse and include everything from ones that merely protect the camcorder lens itself (Skylight filter) to graduated filters that can gradually change colour from clear at the bottom to a colour at the top.

At this stage it's worth remembering that much of what you can do with a lens filter, you can also replicate during the edit in software. If you do it at the software stage you'll be able to edit the effect, tone it up or down or even remove it completely – something you would never be able to do with a lens filter.

*Figs 29–31 – Lights come in many shapes and sizes – on-camera, stand-mounted or hand-held.*

### Filters

Other filters include:

• *Neutral Density:* For reducing the threat of underexposure in bright conditions, and for reducing depth of field.

• *Colour Correcting:* Changes the overall hue of the whole frame.

• *Polarizing:* For eliminating reflections, such as those from mirrors or water. Your camcorder lens has a filter diameter (i.e. 43mm, 37mm) and this helps you select the right size to fit your model. However, it's also possible to buy a Matte box, which clips around your camcorder's lens and allows you to slot in any type of filter.

### Lens Converters

Very useful for grabbing detailed shots, with a difference. Lens converters fall into two categories – teleconverters and wide-angle converters. Teleconverters increase the focal length of your camcorder's lens, zooming into the subject, while wide-angle converters do the opposite, allowing you to shoot in tighter spaces (like inside a car, for example).

As with filters, lens converters fit onto the end of the camcorder lens, and for the more ambitious videomaker there are special converters, such as a fish-eye, which is an ultra-wide conversion lens.

*Figs 32–33 – Sound advice: use the right microphone for the right situation.*

## Lights

You have two options: lights that are on the camcorder (either built-in or ones you attach), or external lights. Lights can be used simply to lift the gloom of a shot, so you can ensure you get detail in the picture. However, they can also be used to add atmosphere. Lighting an interview subject in a certain way can increase tension and intrigue. Likewise in fiction you can evoke the right mood of horror, comedy or drama.

On a camcorder lights have a limited value, so it's better to plump for a small lighting kit, if you are intent on producing high quality results. Accessory companies offer starter kits, which usually include three "redhead" lights – the most generally useful type of light – and perhaps a stand and reflector. The more ambitious your project the more specialist lights you will need. Check our Useful Information section (page 155) for lighting suppliers.

*Fig 34 – Heads up: make sure you hear what is being recorded on tape.*

*Figs 35–36 – Stay secure. Protect your camcorder when it is not in use.*

Alternatively, you can try going for a cobbled-together lighting kit consisting of lights available from your local DIY centre. It's not as glamorous or as controllable; however, it's considerably cheaper.

### Microphone

The purchase of an external mic (make sure your DV cam has an external mic socket) frees you from the shackles of the in-built mic. Two types are available: dynamic and electret. The first requires no battery. A coil attached to its diaphragm is moved by sound waves and vibrates between the poles of a magnet to produce an electronic signal. Ideal for quiet locations, as the mic itself generates little noise, such as interviews and narration. Electret mics need a battery to power a built-in pre-amplifier that consequently boosts the signal. They are powerful and also more sensitive than dynamic mics. Overly loud audio can overload them, and they produce some noise themselves. Within these two types of mic there are several pick up patterns, which show the mic's angle of sound acceptance: **Omnidirectional** – picking up sound equally from all directions; **Cardioid** – sound picked up from the direction the mic is pointing; **Super-cardioid**, **Hypercardioid** – more directional than cardioid, these often reject sounds coming from behind or the side.

### Headphones

Essential for monitoring the sound you are recording. The ear is a sophisticated piece of technology that can filter out the sounds you don't want to hear (insert sexist nagging joke here!). Even expensive mics can't always

do this. Make sure you know what's going down on tape. Ensure your camcorder has an external headphone jack before purchase though.

### Media and Batteries

Small enough to forget yet you'd be lost without them. A supply of whatever media your camcorder uses – be it tapes, memory cards or DVDs, and a selection of charged batteries is essential for any production, whether it be holiday, birthday, fiction or documentary. All media are affordable, more so when bought in bulk. Batteries are more expensive but you should invest in a separate charger and at least one extra battery.

*Fig 37 – The Mini DV tape takes up almost no space.*

## Camcorder Cases and Bags

Think of your camcorder as a vulnerable possession – and make its home a pleasant one. Twee, we know, but it's easy to forget just how much your camcorder cost you. Bags should be heavily padded and have space for plenty of tapes, batteries and accessories. The less ostentatious your carrier, the less likely it is to find itself in a bag marked swag.

## Dollies, Cranes and Track

Bonjour Monsieur Professional! Dollies and cranes offer videomakers the chance to get incredible footage. However, it comes at a cost. You need to ensure you have a use for these expensive goodies. Dollies are "vehicles" that can be pushed along a plastic or metal track in order to follow action – hence the phrase tracking shot. But dollies don't need to be pro set-ups they can be any wheeled platform that allow the camcorder and its operator to keep up with the subject.

Wheelchairs and prams are often used in amateur shoots, but for the budget-conscious professional there are also very useable dollies designed to use a standard ladder or even hosepipes as tracks. Basic tripod mounted jibs (long arms for high, swinging shots) are also available for £100–300. Unless you're intent on recreating the crowd scenes from *Gladiator,* it might be worth keeping cranes to your bigger productions. Excellent for sweeping ground to air shots, or shots from extreme angles, these are costly and need a team of operators, plus an external monitor to view what you're shooting.

*Fig 38 – Supports such as dollies provide interesting shots as in* Gladiator *(2000).*

# THE BASICS

# THE BASICS

THE BASICS

**D**espite the prolific number of camcorder designs available to consumers, there are many key functions which are incorporated (to varying degrees) on all models. Here we have listed the most common buttons and controls you will find your fingers heading towards, along with a description of what they do and whether they are any good or not!

### AUTOMATIC SETTINGS

All digital camcorders, whether they are expensive or cheap, include automatic functions, which are activated as soon as you turn the camcorder's power on. This is where the term **point and shoot** comes from, as these auto settings take control over focus, exposure levels, white balance and shutter speeds. The videomaker therefore has nothing to do but point the camcorder in the direction of the action and press the big red record button!

While the sophistication of automatic systems has increased, the level of performance can fluctuate, and relying totally on auto pilot often results in footage which, while acceptable, could be so much better. In many cases, the automatic systems simply cannot reproduce the shot you are after. Examples of this include shooting in low light conditions, starting to shoot indoors and then moving outdoors, as well as pull focus shots.

In low light the digital camcorder's circuitry boosts the DV signal in order to add detail to the picture. Therefore, when it is dark or gloomy, the camcorder tries to increase the light. This is often referred to as **gain,** or **gain-up.** Unfortunately, when it is trying to increase detail, the camcorder only promotes picture noise (grain) and the quality of the image degrades.

Capturing the right kind of light is very difficult. Our eyes are sophisticated at reading colour, camcorders are not, and can easily be tripped up by changes in colour. Most of what we see is a result of reflected light, i.e. not many objects generate their own light (the sun and artificial light being the main "sources"), and therefore the colour of an object is dependent on the colour of the light source and its own physical properties. Indoor artificial lights have a yellow/orange cast, while natural light is blue. Moving from one to the other

*Fig 1 – The camcorder will automatically focus on subjects closer to it.*

*Fig 2 – Automatic white balance becomes a problem when mixing light sources.*

using a camcorder's auto white balance setting will result in the colour of objects not always being true, as the camcorder boosts the intensity of colours to compensate for the changes in light.

Auto focus systems can also be hindered by rapid movement. If the camcorder does not have a speedy auto focus, then you will be left waiting a fraction of a second longer than necessary for objects to come into focus – this is commonly known as **hunting.** Using auto focus can also create problems when the subject of your shot is not at the front of the frame. Camcorders will generally concentrate focus on the first substantial object they see, leaving the background of the shot out of focus. In most situations, the auto setting will offer a large depth of field, whereby most of the frame is in focus. However, if, for example, you were shooting with railings or a fence in the foreground then it could prove difficult keeping what is in the background of the shot in focus if you relied totally on the auto focus system.

Pull focus is a common technique used in film and video production. It essentially sees the focus change from one object to another within a sequence of footage. It helps concentrate the audience's attention on what is important, and helps to convey a point without recourse to dialogue. Imagine a wine glass in focus at the front of a shot; gradually the glass goes out of focus and the background comes into focus, revealing a character opening a bottle of wine. It would be impossible to create this shot using auto focus.

## MANUAL FOCUS, EXPOSURE, WHITE BALANCE AND SHUTTER SPEEDS

Manual systems allow you to tell the camcorder what you want to see. Initially this might lead to images that are not exactly what you would expect, but once you become *au fait* with exposure, shutter speeds and white balance, it is possible to get very creative.

Very few digital camcorders lack any manual functions, though many budget models will only include manual focus. Selecting manual focus is usually done by pressing a button on the exterior of the camcorder to engage the mode. The user will then control focus by rotating a manual focus ring around the lens barrel, or a small thumbwheel on the left side, or back, of the camcorder. Manual focus rings are the best system for controlling focus as they are larger and easier to use than thumbwheels, make less noise (which can often be picked up by the camcorder's microphone) and are more sensitive. Unfortunately, it is rare to find focus rings on budget camcorders – they seem to be the preserve of true enthusiast machines. Camcorders with touch sensitive view-screens often also feature "touch-focus" – allowing you to simply touch a portion of the image to make the camcorder focus on that area. This is quick and powerful, but few camcorders offer it. The reasons for using manual focus have been well highlighted in the Automatic Settings section (see page 34).

Seizing control of white balance, exposure and shutter speeds is predominantly done via a DV camcorder's menu system, though a thumbwheel, or selector dial, is used to control the exposure or shutter speed rate.

Using manual exposure and white balance settings allows the user to compensate for light or dark shooting conditions, and, in the case of white balance, to record colour accurately. To make the best of these features, the user needs to control the amount of light entering the lens. Too much light and the picture will be over exposed, too little and it will be under exposed. The camcorder's iris and shutter speeds are essential to this control.

*Fig 3 – Manual controls, such as focus and exposure, allow more shooting flexibility.*

The iris is often referred to as the aperture, and is a round hole behind the lens. To restrict light entering the lens when the conditions are too bright it needs to be closed. If the light is too low, then this aperture needs to be opened to make the most of what light there is. The size of the aperture/iris is measured in numbers known as **f stops.**

Domestic DV camcorders will generally have a wide selection of f stops controlled automatically and manually on entry-level and enthusiast models. Having control over these provides much more flexibility for the user.

As for the shutter, well that is a term picked up from stills photography. The shutter itself is actually an

*Fig 4 – Using auto focus can result in your camera "hunting" for an object to come into focus.*

*Fig 5 – Even tranquil scenes can benefit from careful use of manual controls.*

## Advanced Features

If you're prepared to shell out for a slightly more up-market machine, there are a few extra features you really ought to look out for:

• *Zebras:* Not the lion-fodder variety. In video terms, zebras are one of the most important things to take notice of on your viewscreen. It can be tricky on a 2.5-inch screen to work out when parts of your image are too bright or too dark. Zebra functions will automatically display a striped pattern over any area on your screen which is overexposed allowing you to re-adjust your exposure control to compensate.

• *Levels chart:* Some camcorders can also display a levels chart – basically a little bar graph showing how light is distributed over your picture. Vertical lines indicate the amount of your picture which is bright or dark. Images which have all the lines concentrated at one end of the graph are either two bright or too dark.

• *Audio input:* Make sure your camcorder has a microphone or audio input socket. Adding an extra mic is virtually essential if you want to do anything but the most basic recording. If you get a really posh machine it might have xlr inputs. These are professional audio recording sockets, but for most purposes you can do without them.

• *Audio monitoring:* The ability to display audio levels on-screen as you record means that you can easily keep a check on background sounds or sounds which are likely to distort.

• *Automatic levels adjustment:* Many cameras will automatically adjust the audio levels from an external microphone so that sound is always recorded at the optimum level. This is a useful feature, but it can work against you. If you've got a generally quiet scene with occasional loud noises (like a firework display) the auto function will adjust for the quiet ambience making it too loud and then not be quick enough to stop the loud bangs from distorting. Look for a manual option for recording levels.

• *Zoom-focus:* It's hard to manually focus perfectly on a tiny 2.5-inch screen. Zoom-focus is a little button which, when held down, zooms in on the centre of the screen, allowing you to get the focus right without changing the shot. When you release it, your original framing returns.

• *Macro:* If you're shooting at very close range (filming tiny subjects just a few centimetres from the lens), a macro is the only way to do it. Generally, you can't zoom when the macro is turned on, but it will allow you to focus on very close objects.

• *Accessory shoe:* A square connection on the top of the camcorder which can be used to attach extra lights and microphones.

• *Video inputs:* If your camcorder has firewire, check that it can import as well as export footage – that way you'll be able to archive your finished movies back to tape. Some camcorders even have analogue inputs allowing you to use them to transfer footage from (say) a VCR or DVD to a digital format. If you've got a lot of old analogue camcorder footage, this can be a way to transfer it for editing on your PC or Mac.

*Fig 6 – More powerful cameras often come with on-screen displays like levels and zebras. These help you work out how well lit and balanced your shot is.*

*Fig 7 – The AE menu provides sports mode to capture fast-moving action.*

electronically-controlled device on camcorders, situated behind the aperture. It opens for a split second to let light through and then closes to block it out. The speed at which it does this is known as **shutter speed.**

On domestic DV camcorders the standard shutter speed is 1/50th of a second, but this can be changed with a manual function to speeds in excess of 1/8000th of a second. The benefit of being able to change shutter speeds is seen when you move away from shooting "standard" footage.

Variable shutter speeds are a must for capturing fast-moving action such as motor sport or football. Using a standard 1/50th shutter speed here will result in blurred footage – still sharp, but blurred.

There is a downside to using higher shutter speeds, however. You have altered the amount of light coming through the lens and so you need to be in brightly lit conditions to see the best of it. There is also the problem of jerky footage, as sports footage is often slowed for slow motion replays or blur-free frame-by-frame analysis. Hence camcorder manuals' fondness for pointing out how great high shutter speeds are for improving your tennis serve or golf swing!

Manual white balance might also mean you have to carry a selection of coloured card around with you! Setting white balance manually involves placing the camcorder in the right mode via the menu system, pointing the camcorder at a piece of white card or paper and setting the white balance level. This tells the camcorder what is white – and it then relates the setting of colours to this. However, in order to be more creative, you can "trick" the camcorder by using different shades and colours.

**PROGRAM AE MODES**

Program AE modes are included on all digital camcorders. They are pre-configured auto exposure settings designed to cover the most obvious shooting conditions, such as sports, portrait, landscape, low light, spotlight, sunset, ski and snow.

An easy fix, should your digital camcorder not have too many manual functions, they are either hidden away in the camcorder's menu system or incorporated on a dial on the back, or side, of the camcorder.

**THUMBWHEELS, DIAL AND SELECTORS**

Every camcorder manufacturer has different design

*Fig 8 – On sand or snow, beaches and skis, AE modes help to compensate for extremely bright light.*

criteria, but all make use of thumbwheels, dial and selector switches. The miniaturization of digital technology has meant these controls are smaller than ever before, and can be frustrating to use. Thumbwheels etc., usually control the selection of program AE modes, focus, exposure and digital picture effects.

## TIMECODE

Most video footage in the UK is recorded at 25 frames per second (in the US, it's 30fps and some non-standard video recorders like those in mobile phones can record at 15 or even 10fps). When you get into editing, you'll find each frame is numbered by hours, minutes, seconds and frames, so, for example, one frame of video will be time-coded as 00:15:46:02 and the next frame will be 00:15:46:03. If your recording machine has options, it's best to go for high frame-rates (25 or 30fps) so that movement is smooth and fluid. Some cameras offer a 24fps option. Feature films are shot at 24fps, so if you want that cinematic look, the 24fps setting will help.

## RECORDING BUTTON

Usually the big red button on the back of the camcorder and too obvious to miss. Some camcorders have a protective flap across the record button which needs to be flicked back before the camcorder can be switched on and recording can take place. Other models will have a switch or dial that needs to be moved to "On" before the recording button can be pressed.

## ZOOM

Optical and digital zooms are included on all DV camcorders. Optical systems can run up to 25x magnification, while digital can exceed 700x, but the latter will result in image degradation. Zoom controls are always on the exterior of the camcorder and usually take the form of a lever or a rocker, moved to the left or right (in and out).

It is advisable for the zoom to be used sparingly as it does not look attractive or professional in videos. It is better to zoom in on your subject before pressing record.

*Fig 9 – To make the best use of the zoom feature, zoom in before you press the record button.*

### IMAGE STABILIZATION

Two systems are available – optical and digital (see Buying the Right Camcorder) – and both offer a convenient way of steadying camera shake when you do not have access to a tripod – though this remains the most professional way of achieving smooth footage. Image stabilization can make footage appear jerky. It is located in the camcorder menu system.

### DIGITAL AND PICTURE EFFECTS

Competition within the camcorder market has led to an increasing number of digital effects being included on even the most basic digital camcorders. Essentially, these are gimmicky features which are cheap to include and look enticing, but which have limited practical use.

Typical digital effects include: sepia, negative, classic film, strobe, gain-up, trail, solarize, black and white and mosaic. The effect is selected before shooting and then applied to the footage, i.e. sepia will add a brownish, old fashioned tinge to the video, negative will reverse colours, solarize will enhance colours to give the look of a poster, while mosaic does exactly what it says – and consequently is not used that much!

Hidden away in the menu system, digital picture effects can also include settings such as scene transitions. Fades and wipes can be selected and a scene can therefore be faded in from black or white. Wipes can see the scene start by sliding in from the left, right, top or bottom of the frame.

More advanced digital camcorders in the entry-level and enthusiast sectors allow users to apply digital effects on recorded footage.

If you're planning to use a computer to edit your footage in any way, it's best to ignore in-camera effects entirely. There's never anything in them that can't be done better and more controllably inside the computer, and if you do an effect in-camera, it stays on your shot forever. If you do it on your computer, you can just as easily undo it if you don't like it.

### DIGITAL STILL SNAPSHOT

The line between stills cameras and camcorders

*Fig 10–13 – Adding picture effects, such as negative or mosaic, can give your images a completely different spin.*

continues to blur, with most stills models incorporating video recording and almost all camcorders allowing you to record snapshots to a memory card. Camcorders generally have high quality lenses, but their light sensitive chips are designed for video, so quality is often limited (even HD is much lower quality than most photos). Check the megapixel count for still images and don't be deceived by blurb that speaks vaguely about "high quality stills".

You can transfer still images onto a computer via a USB cable, and many camcorders come with image manipulation software to "play" with the images once they have been transferred onto a computer. PC software is more readily supplied than Mac software.

## NIGHT-SHOOTING FEATURES

Aside from your DV camcorder's ability to shoot in low light conditions, it might also incorporate a near-darkness shooting mode. Sony's system is called NightShot, JVC's NightScope and Panasonic's NightView. Essentially, they all offer the same: recording in very low light conditions. This is beneficial if you are intending to video nocturnal wildlife, use your camcorder as a motion sensor in a security situation, or if you want to get a shot of your child sleeping peacefully at the end of a hectic birthday!

Sony and Panasonic's system uses a short-range, infra-red light. The infra-red lamp is a small

LED mounted on the front of the camera. It gives off no visible light, but will let you take clear shots of anything within 3–4 metres (10–13 feet) of the camera. The lamp does run your battery down slightly faster, but the effect is not huge. This will provide slightly ghoulish, greenish images, with a white effect on the subject's pupils, but shots are generally smooth and focus is good. You can use this system in pitch darkness.

JVC's system makes use of available light so it will provide colour images but, works by exposing each image for longer – meaning camera motion and movement within the shot become very blurry. Frame-rates may also suffer with the frame rate being reduced to just a few frames per second. This system only works in moderately dark conditions and you need to keep the camera steady.

If you want images which are both smooth and colourful, your only option is to light the scene. A light attached to the shoe on top of the camera is often the best solution in this situation, but try to get one that has its own battery or you'll run out of juice very quickly.

**PROGRESSIVE SCAN**
Only available on a limited number of camcorders, Progressive Scan offers a way of capturing sharp, blur-free moving and still images. The fields and frames that make up a single camcorder image are de-interlaced. The resulting image is ideal

*Fig 14 – Because low light conditions add grain to your images, night shooting features can come to your aid.*

*Fig 15 – Carrying out simple maintenance, such as cleaning the lens, will be allowed in the warranty, but do not tinker with the insides!*

for analysis in a frame-by-frame manner, though moving Progressive Scan footage does exhibit jerky movement. Both Canon and Panasonic make use of Progressive Scan on their digital camcorders.

Progressive shooting is often used with High Definition camcorders as it offers exceptional image resolution.

### BASIC CAMCORDER MAINTENANCE

Although you might want this to be the longest section in this book, we are sorry to say it is going to be one of the shortest! Camcorders are intricately engineered and we cannot recommend that you attempt any maintenance yourself.

Mini DV camcorders tend to be even more sophisticated than their analogue counterparts, so we would suggest you always seek the advice of a qualified engineer if your camcorder starts to malfunction. There are

simply so many things that can go wrong on a digital camcorder it is not worth giving yourself sleepless nights over them. The majority of retailers and dealers will offer some kind of repair service, as will all the camcorder manufacturers, if you contact them directly, while there are also independent engineers you can find through the *Yellow Pages*. It is also useful to remember that the internet, through newsgroups and message boards, is an excellent resource, and allows you to converse with like-minded individuals. Remember also that tinkering with your DV camcorder invariably invalidates its warranty, so if you do decide to have just a bit of a fiddle, think about the cost of having to buy a new digital camcorder, as opposed to the cost of having one repaired!

### TAKE PRECAUTIONS

Although tinkering with your camcorder is not recommended, there are several precautions you can take to limit what might go wrong. These range from the obvious to the still-fairly-obvious-but-very-easy-to-forget!

Generally, today's camcorders are pretty robust. However, knocks and bumps can damage the mechanisms. Camcorders recording to memory cards are exceptionally tough. With no moving parts they can't be easily damaged and if you're trying

*Fig 16 – A padded bag is a secure way of transporting your valuable equipment.*

*Fig 17–18 – Widening the horizons. New technology in television means that widescreen will soon become the normal viewing medium.*

to video extreme sports, they could be your best choice. For DV, DVD and hard disk camcorders, try to ensure you have a heavily padded pouch or case for your camcorder to protect it while you are travelling with it.

Whatever your system, buy either a lens cloth, or brush, from a camera manufacturer to remove small dust and dirt particles from the lens. The lens is one of the most important parts of your camcorder: help to preserve it.

If you have been shooting in the rain, even with a rain jacket covering the camcorder, make sure you leave the camcorder to "dry out" at home, before recording or playing back footage. Condensation has proved to be the cause of a large number of faults.

Reading the technical specifications of your digital camcorder (as you do!), you will often see details concerning the camcorder's operating temperature. Manufacturers, to cover themselves, suggest that camcorders should not be used in extreme conditions: hot, cold or damp. However, it is possible to use digital camcorders in these conditions, provided you are careful with them. Make sure you take protective covers and rain jackets where necessary, and try to avoid going quickly from one extreme situation to another.

Perhaps the best precaution you can take with your digital camcorder is to have it insured. Check with your home contents insurance provider to see if your camcorder is covered, needs adding, or requires a separate policy. As with many insurance policies, make sure you read the small print to ensure your camcorder is covered for trips abroad, as well as at home.

## A FEW WORDS ABOUT SCREEN SHAPES AND IMAGE RESOLUTIONS

Back in the days when the only place for video was a standard television screen there was only one

Fig 19–20 – Seven Samurai *(above) and* Lawrence of Arabia *(below) are often praised for their epic scale and brilliant composition, despite their very different Aspect Ratios (1.37:1 and 2.20:1, respectively).*

shape for a video picture – the TV shape with its 4:3 ratio (4 centimetres (1.5 inches) across for every 3 centimetres (1 inch) down and 720x576 pixels as the resolution of the images. Today, the majority of new televisions are widescreen (with a 16:9 ratio), with most video projects being shot specifically for this format and most camcorders being designed for it. High definition images are always 16x9. There are a range of resolutions for High Definition work, but 1440x1080 (often described as 1080i) is the most common.

With the rise of the web as a broadcast medium, there's no longer any reason why your finished video needs to be a particular shape, and many non-standard video devices like web-cams, mobiles, and stills cameras record non-standard shaped images. However, most still opt for 16:9 or 4:3 (with 640x480 pixels being a common resolution).

You can also mess about with resolutions in the edit, but it's far easier to scale down footage recorded at too high quality than it is to scale up low quality work, so always record at the best quality your machine will allow, and make sure you get a machine with the highest resolution you can.

Of course, this rule becomes more difficult to follow when you're using a hard-disk- or memory-card-based machine. The higher the quality of the footage, the more space it will use up and the quicker you'll run out of memory, so be realistic about the shooting you plan to do and make sure you have enough space to store everything you need.

*Fig 21 – A narrow picture area evolved on older televisions due to limited technology.*

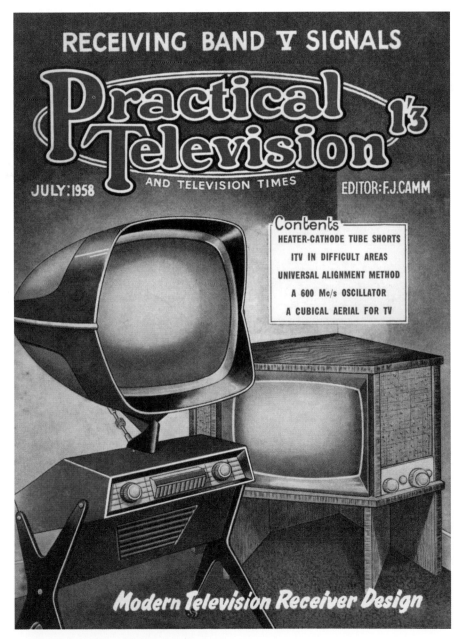

SKIL

# SKILLS

# SKILLS

SKILLS

## COMPOSITION

Proper composition is an invaluable aid to videomaking, and should be regarded as much a tool as a tripod or video light. Careful thought about the layout of your shot, what will be in it and where it will be, can make an incredible difference both to the look of your film and to the feelings your images convey.

If composition was not vital, then Orson Welles would never have ripped up the floorboards to get a worm's eye camera angle on Charles Kane, communicating the man's imposing presence in a way that renders dialogue unnecessary.

As if composition was not important enough as a storytelling tool, then it is worth remembering that badly composed shots can ruin a good film – it may seem like a good joke to position someone so that the trees in the background appear to be sprouting from your subject's scalp, but in fact it is little more than a bad pun, at best a distraction and at worst an amateurish mistake.

Fortunately, there are rules and guidelines you can follow in order to create well-composed shots. For a dramatic videographer telling a fictional story, there will be time to plan shots with these rules in mind, for a documentary maker capturing video on-the-fly, good composition will not always be possible. The rules, however, will become second nature very quickly, and even if pushed a good videographer will be able to apply them

*Fig 1 – Good composition is one of the many reasons why* Citizen Kane *is hailed as one of the greatest and most influential films ever made.*

*Fig 2 – An asymmetrical composition usually looks better than allowing your subject to dominate the frame.*

instinctively. Of course, once you have this much grasp of the rules you can begin trying creatively to break them!

## Think Ahead

Early planning is helpful both for avoiding common composition mistakes and for getting the best out of your location – it is vital to know what you want to shoot in order to make sure you shoot it correctly. Having established a list of things you wish to commit to tape, you can work out where you will position the cam for a "safety" or master shot and figure out what other shots you will need and what they are supposed to accomplish.

Knowing what your shot is intended to convey will help you plan its composition – there is no point having a shot in your finished work that is simply there because you had it on tape. Knowing that the subject of a shot needs to appear menacing, or dynamic, or serene will help you work out how the shot must be composed.

When you get to your location, try to see the shot the way your camcorder will: look for unlit objects, size discrepancies, obstructive items of scenery, things that are eyecatchingly bright and just about anything that will call unwanted attention to itself. Items like this are an inconvenience only if they go unnoticed until you have already shot. If you check things out beforehand you can turn annoyances into advantages – the obstructive branch right in the middle of the frame can be turned into useful foreground interest with a quick repositioning of the camcorder.

## Rule of Thirds

Having disposed of, utilized or worked around potential troublespots, you can begin composing the shot with the camera. The most important guideline in composition is the rule of thirds, a guide that constantly comes in handy by making your shots look well balanced via the odd method of deliberately putting them together along unbalanced lines.

The most important item in any shot does not necessarily have to be at the centre of the frame. In actual fact, short of attempting to dominate an entire shot, it is generally best to avoid placing your subject dead centre as it will prevent your viewer from being able to relate anything else in the shot to the actual subject.

Imagine a shot of a landscape with the horizon falling dead centre across the screen – are you supposed to be paying attention to the land or to the sky? Instead, try to allocate two thirds of a frame to one part of the shot and the other third to the remainder. Imagine the screen divided into thirds across the horizontal and vertical in a grid – the intersections of these gridlines are usually the best place to position your subject.

Using the rule of thirds, composition will provide a natural-looking asymmetry to your footage rather than a staged and arranged look. Additionally, it serves to draw the viewers attention to where it needs to be whilst allowing the subject, foreground and background to complement, rather than compete with, each other.

### Perspective and Points of View

Another point to keep in mind when filming is the nature of the medium – there is no point filming the three-dimensional real world and expecting it to have depth when played back on your 2D TV screen – you have to create the depth yourself.

Perspective problems can easily be solved with a little thought about camera placement. Extra depth or better perspective can be added to a shot simply by engineering it so as to avoid common pitfalls and make use of the available space.

Think of a tall skyscraper – a common mistake is to film it head on. It is an understandable error: filling the screen with the subject seems like a good way of conveying the building's scale and presence, but you will find that, rather than dominating the shot, the undynamic presentation of the building will make it seem as imposing as a pile of bricks.

To make the scale of the building more apparent you should drag your camera to one of its corners and shoot from there – automatically adding a vanishing point to your shot as the facade of the building recedes into the distance and allowing other items into the shot to give a sense of relative sizes.

*Figs 3–4 – A dramatic camera angle and a bit of foreground interest make these shots much more dramatic than a simple head-on perspective could.*

*Fig 5 – A naturally occurring frame can make your images much more interesting, while providing contrast.*

Another trick using the example of a building is to place your camera near the foot of the building and shoot upwards. The change of angle will allow the building to loom overhead and with careful framing you will get a natural border of sky which will start off narrow and widen as distance "shrinks" the building – the dwindling upper floors of the building combined with the expanding frame of sky will impart the size of the building effectively, and the more dramatic the effect the more visual representation of size you will get.

Looming buildings are just an example, of course. These rules can be applied to pretty much anything. People, however, may object to having their double chins in shot as you crouch at their feet shooting upwards, and shooting from the side may make them uncomfortable, especially in drama, where actors have to appear ignorant of the camera's presence – they know you are there, they know you are doing something, but they are not allowed to look. Not knowing what is going on may cause self-conscious subjects to cast sidelong glances at your cam. That is not to say you cannot shoot people using these

methods, but it may be better to experiment with other methods, especially if your subjects are saying or doing things that will not be picked up from low or diagonal angles.

Adding foreground interest is a good way of adding perspective to a picture where clever camera angles cannot be used. Simply relocate the camera to incorporate a naturally occurring object in the foreground or add a prop to accomplish the same effect. This has the added advantage of allowing you, if necessary, to drag the viewer's attention from object to subject by opening up the depth of field or doing a quick focus pull.

If you can't find a suitable foreground object for some reason (say there is nothing, or what is available would be too distracting) then try moving your subject to somewhere that provides a naturally occurring frame. This way you can add interest and a sense of scale to your shot without having any distractions in the foreground. Doorways, bridges, a corridor of trees, all of these will naturally frame your subject, drawing attention to the relevant part of the image in a pleasing, but non-distracting, way.

The naturally occurring frame has another bonus to it should you want to play cute with your footage – it allows you to manipulate contrast levels within the picture. An internal shot of a doorway can provide a dark border to a sunlit street, whilst an external shot through a doorway into a darkened interior can add a touch of menace to an image.

Natural frames also provide another way of messing with your audience's perceptions, albeit in a risky fashion. Say, for example, you have a distant building and you frame it through the legs of a stone seat – with careful planning the shot can look as if it has been taken through a massive archway rather than through a narrow space – meaning that objects appearing in the mid-ground between frame and subject will appear to be out of proportion with their surroundings. This sort of gimmick can add novelty value to your shots but should be handled carefully – the line between amusing trick and terribly misjudged shot is a thin one, and one that is easily crossed.

Speaking of crossing lines, do not. This is another rule as fundamental as the rule of thirds. Say for example you have two people talking to each other, one on the left of the screen, the other on the right. Imagine a line drawn between them – should you shoot from one side of the line and then shoot from the opposite side your subjects will appear to have swapped sides despite not having moved. This will be noticed by your audience and will instantly shatter their illusions. Either pick a side and stick to it, shoot the conversation using "over-the-shoulder" shots or carefully combine the two using the shot of both subjects as a safety and over-the-shoulder shots as inserts.

Not crossing the line in a simple, two-person shot is fairly simple, but becomes more complicated when extra people are added. Think of the diner scene in *Reservoir Dogs*, or the post-trial pub gathering in *Trainspotting*. Both scenes are fairly minor in terms of their importance to the overall story, but try watching those films with a gaggle of film buffs and those scenes will invariably draw

*Fig 6 – When filming a conversation, make sure you don't "cross the line".*

comment for the way they handle conversations between large groups of people without accidentally crossing the line in an attempt to get the relevant speakers in shot.

Careful planning of group shots can be a subtle way of drawing appreciative comment from savvy fans, but it is also a minefield for the unwary and requires meticulous planning to get it right. Think about where your speakers and addressees are sitting, the order in which different people will speak their lines and where your camera will be placed for the very first shot. That is the point where the first of many "lines" will be established and the place you have to build the rest of the scene from. Draw a diagram of the scene to plan things out. If you are filming from the head of a table and are starting with a conversation between two people opposite each other before moving on to

*Fig 7 – Working out a shot diagram based on the order of dialogue in your script can help avoid mistakes, especially where it comes to scenes set at the dinner table!*

a conversation between people side by side, you will have to move your camera to the opposite side of the table, to avoid having one subject obscured by another. This is where you might cross the line. There is no way around these risks apart from painstaking shot planning. Even with pre-planning make sure you have a safety take and inserts ready so that any disaster with your bravura crowd scene can be rescued in the edit suite by substituting a more conventional approach to group conversations.

### MP-Movement

Moving objects also require careful composition, mainly to avoid glaring mistakes that will upset your audience's ability to immerse themselves in your drama or distract them from the points you are trying to make in a documentary.

Always allow for both moving and looking room within your shots – we have all been annoyed by a bad mime act doing a naff "walking-against-the-wind"

*Fig 8 – Moving
subjects will need
space to move into.*

performance. That is the effect you will achieve if you don't allow room in your shots for events to happen. If you are panning or dollying alongside a walking person or moving car then allow them room to move into. A car moving from left to right across the screen should be framed with space to its right and this space should be kept until the point when the camera movement stops, allowing the car to move naturally out of shot. Should you fail to allow enough room the car will run into the edge of the screen and the sideways movement of the camera will look as if it is being "pushed" by the car. Rule of thirds can be used to great effect here – line up a right-moving object on the left-hand thirds and you will avoid the push effect and will not appear as though you are struggling to keep pace with the subject.

Try to avoid too many cuts in a shot featuring moving subjects – allowing a subject to progress partway across the screen and then cutting to a later shot where the movement is even more advanced will provide a noticeable and annoying jump in the action, a jump cut. Should a movement be taking too long to complete try fading slowly between cuts to truncate the shot in a much more artistic and less jarring fashion.

Moving room also applies to slower shots such as someone walking toward the camera – if you fail to allow space between their feet and the bottom of the screen they will appear to be walking on thin air – make sure they have some foreground to walk into.

Slower movements require even more careful composition. A simple left to right framing of a moving object is fine for conveying that object's speed, but something that moves more slowly will lack dynamism as it moves flatly across the scene without any change in perspective. Try using a diagonal composition – a person enters a room at the top left and moves diagonally to exit bottom right, allowing them to grow in stature as they approach the camera and giving your audience the chance to examine the subject head on.

*Fig 9 – Remember to stay just ahead of the subject, especially if you are trying to give your audience a feel for speed.*

*Fig 10 – This toddler may be very upset at his parent's recent decapitation! Frame your shots carefully.*

### Unnecessary Amputations

Speaking of heads, remember to allow headroom for people in shots. Be it an immaculate £300 haircut or the mullet from hell you have no business cutting off people's hair. Frame head-shots with a noticeable gap between the top of someone's head and the top of the image to avoid an amateurish mistake. Alternatively, should you be going for a big close-up on a subject's face that makes some loss of the subject inevitable, then try to cut off a significant amount, making the close-up much larger and ensuring that any loss of the subject is clearly deliberate.

The rule of thirds makes itself useful here yet again – the most important part of any headshot is usually the eyes – place them on the uppermost line of your rule of thirds grid and you will have a well-balanced and natural-looking image without chopping off the head or the other alternative of leaving too much headroom and causing your subject to look pint-sized.

Similarly, try to avoid shots that cut people off across naturally occurring joints, a person framed with the bottom of the image cutting off across their waist will look like they have had a nasty accident. Try to make the edges of your image fall across limbs partway between joints – cut off at mid-thigh rather than at the knees, for example.

Weightings are another important part of composition, and a very subtle part at that. All items and locations have different effects on the eye, and these effects can be assessed and exploited. Warm colours, such as red and orange, will attract the viewer's eye more effectively than colder blues and whites. The placing of objects also carries a certain weight – pick up an advertising directory and check out the most expensive areas of a page you can buy – you will soon notice that top right-hand spots are the most coveted and highly priced because the eye naturally tends to fall in that location. This rule is less true with a moving screen image than a static page, but it still applies to a certain extent, and should be kept in mind.

Most rules of composition are there for one of two reasons – to add a dramatic visual element to your story, or to avoid a visual trick that will disrupt your audience's ability to suspend disbelief. Like all rules in videomaking, there are times when the rules can be broken to good effect, but it takes an experienced eye to know when to do so. In general, it is better to be safe than sorry, so if you are going to break the rules then make sure you know what rules you are breaking and why, before you risk throwing away a perfectly good scene for the sake of some experimental framing that may not pay off. Imitation is good, but you are better safe than shoddy!

*Figs 11–12 – Colour can affect the "warmth" of a shot and the feeling it conveys to the viewer. Compare the warm reds in a desert and the cold blues and whites in this glacial scene.*

*Fig 13 – Warning: cigarettes can seriously damage your continuity. Drifting smoke and changing cigarette lengths can be the bane of editing.*

## SHOOTING

It is odd to think that when creating a film, a visual story, that your visuals are, to a certain extent, subordinate to a separate part of the process, but it is true. Everything you shoot should have the edit in mind.

That is not to say that what you record on tape is just raw material for the editor. Far from it, getting good shots is what camerawork is all about. There are many elements that constitute a good shot and sometimes even an experienced camera operator will forget, in the heat of composition and framing, that one of those elements is editing.

The footage get on tape should not only provide the excellent visuals needed to tell your story, they should also provide you with the elements you need to tell your story artistically. Your script only outlines the plot and dialogue, your storyboard only establishes certain shots. The gaps missed by the script and storyboard are where a good editor makes his or her mark. Watch any scene in a film and you will see that it is composed of numerous shots, from numerous angles, with various cut-aways or inserts to cover them. Work out the average shot length for a scene and you will see how many short shots a scene is composed from.

A skilled editor will put this collection of shots together in such a subtle fashion that the audience will not notice them as the scene unfolds. It is your job as camera operator to provide the raw materials for this and if, as is often the case, you're the editor as well, you'll soon become acutely aware of how difficult it is to cut footage in which a vital shot is missing or unusable.

On a simple level, this means that the footage you shoot should contain more than just the shots marked out in the storyboard. If you are using expensive film it can be extremely nerve wracking trying to balance the cost against the amount of coverage you think you will need, but this is video, and tape, disk and memory card space are cheap. If you want to make sure you have options in the edit then keep rolling. As long as you exercise enough self control, by forcing your cast and crew through millions of unnecessary

*Figs 14–17 – The distance and framing of a shot can be the difference between an image that sets a scene, such as those on the left, and an image that provides important detail, such as those on the right.*

takes (and remember – everything you shoot has to be watched over and over during the edit – making the whole process longer), you cannot go wrong. Try to keep in mind three things:

*1. Get a master shot.* Say you have a conversation that is going to unfold through various two shots of the actors and a selection of cut-aways. You could just do the various camera set-ups needed to capture the elements of the scenes, but this would be very short-sighted.

Anything that goes wrong with the lighting, the continuity or the technical aspects could render vital footage unusable. If you have a master take of the whole scene either as a long or medium, depending on how much framing is needed, then you always have something to fall back on in the edit. If the worst comes to the worst, it is even possible to use the entire master with some generic cut-aways. Having a master shot covers your back.

*2. Motivation:* Editing does not mean cutting blindly, randomly deciding to curtail shot 1 here and go to shot 2 there. In general, every shot change needs to have a motivation in order to look natural. We are not necessarily talking about a big dramatic moment or movement, we are talking about a simple thing. Imagine that a character is shown in medium profile and you wish to cut to a close-up of his face.

You could just get the two shots and cut them together, but that would merely be two rather static shots joined together. Instead, try to capture the images up to a point that provides a logical reason to cut from one shot to the next. It could be as simple as a flicker of the eyes, a noise from offscreen or something more elaborate such as the lighting of a cigarette. In any case you need some moment that will not overpower the content of the shot, but will be noticeable enough to provide a reason to cut.

*Fig 18 – The subjects in a long shot are recognizable.*

*3: Advancement:* Advancement is simple. In the same way that each scene of your film advances the plot or adds subtle shadings to characterization, each shot should offer the same advancement to the scene it is contained within. You are not simply adding shots in order to keep the scene from being static and boring, you are adding them in order to enhance the scene itself. If you have a character smoking a cigarette, are they taking deep satisfying drags or short, quick nervous ones? Do they neatly tap their ash into the ashtray or are they insolently staining the carpet? You do not want to use shots so blatantly that they telegraph their meaning, but at the same time think about the way in which each shot is telling the miniature story of that scene. Think how the person in shot is to be portrayed and make sure that the shots you take capture the essence of this, so as to visually build the scene from a natural start to a natural finish in accordance with the overt meanings of the screenplay. If you're making a factual programme, the same rules apply. You're still telling a story and even a simple interview provides opportunities for different shots illustrating different ideas and themes and for cut-aways which add colour to your interviewee's background, or illustrate their personality.

## Shot Types

As a film/documentary maker you are already a visual person and can see pictures in your head of how you want things to look. You will have used these pictures to create your storyboard and amend your script. This is all very well when you are merely clarifying things for yourself, but sooner or later you have to explain what you want to the crew, so it is important to get an idea of the definitions of the shots and the forms they take so that you are not saying: "Two guys head to head, we cannot see below their necks, but their faces are really angry and we are over here not over there" when what you need to say is: "A big close-up profile two shot."

There are various terms used to describe the type, angle and content of the shot and you can combine them in any number of ways, for example H/A XLS, which would be a high angle extra long shot. Terms can also be combined with movements of your pan and tilt head or dolly. Below is an outline of the most commonly used shot types, their meaning and their abbreviations used in shot planning, storyboard and shooting script. We will assume, for the sake of simplicity, that the subject of all these shots is a person and that the compositional rules for head and foot room have been properly taken into account.

*Extreme Long Shot (ELS):* The person is so far in the distance that they are only just recognizable as a figure, with no discernible detail.

*Very Long Shot (VLS):* The subject is now close enough to take up approximately half the height of the screen from head to toe. You can probably make out a few more details such as clothes and gender and maybe, if the subject is familiar, identity.

*Long Shot (LS):* From head to toe the person now takes up almost the full height of the screen with the exception of the head and foot room that is left available as part of the composition.

*Medium Long Shot (MLS):* The subject is now framed so that they are cut off just below the knees. They are recognizable and their activities are discernible.

*Medium Shot (MS):* Now framed from just below the waist upward, the person is close enough to fully convey moods and the fine details of activity without having to "play to the balcony".

*Medium Close-up (MCU):* Framed from the chest up, the actions carried out by the character are most likely lost out of shot, but their expression is fully readable and they have begun to dominate the shot.

*Close-up (CU):* Framed from the tops of the shoulder upwards, the audience is now on very intimate terms with the subject, picking up a massive range of facial expression and possibly feeling intimidated, attracted etc, according to the portrayal of the character.

*Big Close-up (BCU):* The subject is now dominating the screen, framed from chin to hairline. Simple movements and expressions now begin to seem exaggerated and the effect is good for conveying powerful emotions.

*Extreme Close-up (ECU):* Now framed from just below the nose to just above the eyebrows. This shot should only be used in carefully selected circumstances as the slightest flicker of the eyes is incredibly exaggerated. Can powerfully convey emotions or simple dominance of surroundings, but is equally likely to descend into unwanted parody.

*Profile:* This is a shot taken from the side of the subject rather than head on.

*¾ Profile:* This a very naturalistic shot taken from a point approximately three-quarters of the way around the 90 degree angle between head on and profile. Especially useful for conveying depth or creating the impression that the subject is paying attention to something unseen offscreen.

*The Two Shot (2S):* This implies that there are two people in the frame and is used in three different ways. The most common is the over-the-shoulder-2s which is used in conversation, usually with a roughly three-quarter profile to take in the back and side of the nearer person facing away from the cam with the other person next to them but further away. The other variations are the profile two shot, which features the two people directly facing each other, and the camera off at the side capturing a profile. Remember not to cross the line when using this. Finally there is the to-camera-two-shot, used if you have to people speaking directly to camera placed side by side and shot head on. Remember that variations in height and... ahem... weight can make these types of shots look comedic if composed improperly. If all else fails, bite the bullet and get the shorter person to stand on a box.

Lastly you have your multitude of camera angles, all of which can essentially be reduced to variations of extremity on the following:

*Fig 19–20 – Profile 2 shots can be used to show people in their surroundings (below) or, conversely, isolate them (bottom).*

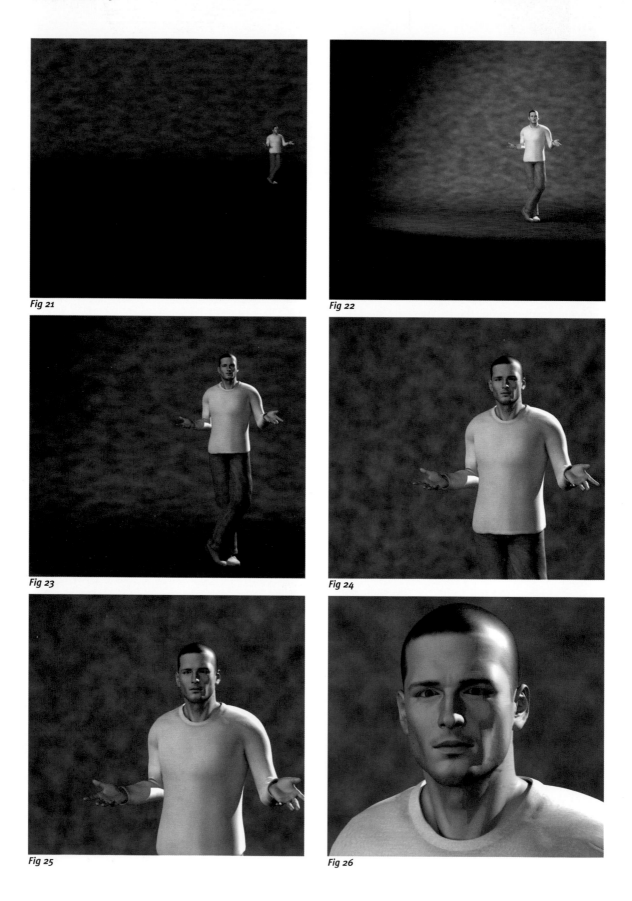

Fig 21

Fig 22

Fig 23

Fig 24

Fig 25

Fig 26

Fig 27

Fig 28

Fig 29

Fig 30

Fig 31

*Fig 21–31 – Shot types:*
*Fig 21 – Extreme Long Shot (ELS)*
*Fig 22 – Very Long Shot (VLS)*
*Fig 23 – Long Shot (LS)*
*Fig 24 – Medium Long Shot (MLS)*
*Fig 25 – Medium Shot (MS)*
*Fig 26 – Medium Close-up (MCU)*
*Fig 27 – Close-up (CU)*
*Fig 28 – Big Close-up (BCU)*
*Fig 29 – Extreme Close-up (ECU)*
*Fig 30 – ³/₄ Profile*
*Fig 31 – Profile 2 Shot, Close (P2SC)*

*Fig 32–34 – The movies*
Se7en *(1995, right),* Vanilla
Sky *(2001, below), and* Black
Narcissus *(1947, below right),*
*all make dramatic and innovative*
*use of lighting.*

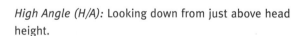

*High Angle (H/A):* Looking down from just above head height.

*Low Angle (L/A):* Looking up from just below shoulder height.

*Bird's Eye:* Looking straight down from above.

*Worm's Eye:* Looking upwards from floor level.

You do not really need to quote an angle if the shot takes place at a level approximating that which you get from your own eyeballs. However, it is worth remembering that there are various subtle variations of this. These include **Point Of View** (POV) shots, which are from a normal height, but generally include a certain amount of movement and rhythm to create the illusion that they are views from a character's eye rather than the camera, and fly-on-the-wall. This is really a term for an overall style, but is occasionally used to imply a high angle wide shot from just below ceiling level.

## LIGHTING

It is so easy to forget, amid all the technical innovation of digital, that light is one of a videomaker's most powerful tools. Used with care and consideration it can raise the quality of a video production.

Light alters an audience's perception of a scene, whether that be in a fiction video, documentary or an interview situation. Even in holiday or wedding videos, light can be used to suggest different moods and feelings.

Learning about light and lighting is worth a book in itself. That is why any self-respecting television programme or film features a lighting cameraman in its credits, whose sole job it is to create the mood and lighting effects the director wants. On large productions you will often see the term **Director of Photography** (DoP) or **Cinematographer;** these are creative people who work with a director to shape the way a film or TV show looks. The best way to understand what a DoP does is to turn yourself into a part-time Media Studies student and just watch lots of movies and videos!

*Fig 35 – Learn to use light and light sources for practical and artistic purposes.*

*Fig 36 – Colour temperature is measured in degrees Kelvin (°K). This diagram shows some typical measurements.*

There are many famous DoPs and Cinematographers, among them Jack Cardiff *(Black Narcissus)*, Darius Khondji *(Se7en)*, Roger Deakins (Coen Brothers movies including *The Man Who Wasn't There* and *Fargo)* and John Toll *(The Thin Red Line, Vanilla Sky)* who paint with light to help ensure the movies retain their silver screen magic. However, they also help push the boundaries of what we see on film, as working with special effects teams they can create highly stylised environments for films such as *Blade Runner* or *Moulin Rouge,* or even *Saving Private Ryan* (where cinematographer Janusz Kaminski removed the protective coating from the camera lens to help provide a bleached out, more realistic look for the film).

Lighting is not only the preserve of these masters of the art; lighting design can be achieved on the most modest of budgets and by the least experienced videomaker. What follows is a little taster of how...

**Light Sources**

As mentioned earlier in this book, there are only two forms of light source – natural and artificial. However, there are a myriad of choices for lighting within these two forms and getting the right one, or the correct blend of lighting, is where the skill part (or you could call it trial and error) comes in.

To achieve a realistic, well-balanced lighting design for your video, you first need to ensure your digital camcorder knows what colour light actually is, in

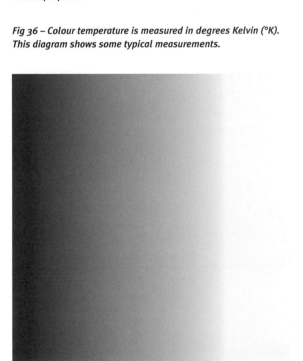

*Figs 37–40 – There are only two light sources: natural and artificial. Difficulties for videomakers occur when the two are mixed.*

order for it to assume that light is white. You do this by setting the white balance – sadly, for those of you without this feature on your DV camcorder, you will have to rely on the auto white balance system.

A knowledge of colour temperature is also handy when you are working with light, as you will discover there is a natural order to the sources we use. Colour temperature is measured in degrees Kelvin (°K), and to give you an idea, a candle is measured at around 1,900°K, a light bulb at 2,500°K, normal daylight at 5,500°K and a bright sunlit sky at 10,000°K. Unfortunately for videomakers these sources do not keep to themselves and will often appear together within your camcorder's viewfinder, causing you production problems. Mixed lighting, as it is known, is apparent when you stand by a window in the office, while the office lighting is on. Therefore the "blue" state of natural light is being mixed with the orange/red of artificial light. Depending on how you have the camcorder's white balance set-up, you will get a mixture of accurate and inaccurate colours. Setting it up it set up for daylight will leave the outside light correctly balanced, but will leave the interior shots with oversaturated colours in the orange/red spectrum. Set up for indoor light, and though the office will be balanced correctly, any sign of the outside world will have a distinctly blue cast. Your options for relief here involve filter sheets. You can either cover the window with orange/red filtering sheets and balance the camcorder for artificial light, or perhaps choose to cover the artificial lights with a blue filter and go for a daylight white balance on your camcorder.

While colour temperature is measured in °K, and light output is measured in lumens, illumination is measured in lux. Another glance at your digital camcorder manual will highlight the minimum lux (illumination) figure your model will operate at. This is only a guide figure; be warned, the lower the illumination the more grain (noise) you will see on the picture – and hence one of the main reasons to use lighting.

One lux is actually the amount of light falling on an area – 1 metre$^2$ (11 feet$^2$), 1 metre (3 feet) from the source of one lumen. In practice, the inside of a house is no more than 200 lux, an overcast sky no more than 10,000 lux, while a bright sunny day will register at around 100,000 lux.

**LUX LEVEL CHART**

| Lux Level | Description |
| --- | --- |
| 100,000 | Bright, sunny day |
| 50,000 | |
| 20,000 | |
| 10,000 | Overcast sky |
| 5000 | |
| 3000 | |
| 2000 | |
| 1000 | |
| 300 | |
| 200 | House interior |
| 50 | |
| 20 | Street lighting |
| 10 | |

## TYPES OF LIGHTING

So far we have only dealt with light sources around us, daylight and the artificial lights that surround us, office and home lights, street lights etc. The whole shooting match only gets more complicated as the videomaker introduces his or her own lighting system. Film and television productions will usually employ a sophisticated array of lights, or **luminaires** as they are sometimes known, while the amateur videomaker realistically has three choices of light: on-camcorder; handheld; or stand-mounted.

On-camcorder lights can either be built-in to the camcorder or attached via an accessory shoe. Power is supplied by a battery (in some cases) which fits into the light, or from the camcorder's own battery pack. Either way these lights provide little flexibility and their output is harsh and lacks directionality.

Much better are the second and third options. Handheld lights are far more powerful, can be run from the mains or a battery system, and can be positioned wherever they are needed. Provided, of course, that you have an extra crew member on hand to hold them!

Stand-mounted lights are invariably available in packs: a selection of two or three lights is offered, stands are included, and you might also get a diffuser or reflector for your troubles as well. Very similar to the lights used in professional productions, stand-mounted lights use mains power and offer the most versatility in lighting designs.

Within these second and third categories of lights we will find a diverse selection of illumination to cover all the most obvious lighting scenarios.

*Fig 41 – Stand-mounted lights offer more power and versatility.*

### Floodlight, Spotlight and Softlights

Two terms have been devised to describe the width of the beam provided by lights: floodlight and spotlight. The first provides a wider angle, sometimes up to 90°, but generally around 60°. Spotlight is a far narrower beam, typically being around 20 to 30°.

In looking at these two terms, it is very important to know the role that distance plays with light. Floodlights are usually placed closer to the subject or area, because light intensity diminishes with distance. Spotlights, due to their narrower beam, can direct light over a greater distance.

By far the most common light is the focusing reflector, though you will more normally hear it referred to as a **redhead.** Redheads are powerful lights that can be used both as floodlights and spotlights, courtesy of their directional beam. Even with its capacity as a floodlight, the redhead is often used as a key light, the main ingredient in any set-up, as it provides shape and texture. This is to allow another type, a softlight, to be used. Softlights provide an overall level of light for a scene and also help to fill-in the shadows which are created by floodlights and spotlights.

Other specific types of light used in more professional situations, typically a studio set-up, include beam, sealed-beam and cyc lights.

Modern camcorders are good at dealing with light and getting better. They can operate at a growing

*Fig 42 – Hand-held lights are useful when time is at a premium.*

range of light levels and produce good images with a wide variety of light sources. This means that it's now quite acceptable to be a lot more experimental and creative with your lighting. A set of three redheads will set you back about £1,000. However, pop down to your local DIY centre and you'll find a selection of lighting solutions (some even with tripods) from about £5. Properly handled and with some diffusing foam to soften their effect, these can give you a basic lighting set-up (although they aren't as controllable as professional film lights).

### Reflectors

While not strictly lights, reflectors are probably the most effective (and cheapest) way to lift and manipulate the light in your scene. Simply a disc of coloured fabric about 1 metre (3 feet) across and stretched over a hoop which can be folded neatly into a small light bag, a reflector simply reflects (or absorbs) the light already in your scene. Usually stuck to a tripod or wall or simply held by a helper just off camera, the reflector can be used to fill in shadows, lift dark areas or block out light where it's not wanted. Most reflectors come with coverings in white (for creating soft, diffused light) silver (for harsher light) gold (for creating a warm glow) and black (for creating shadows or limiting light). At just a few pounds each, they never break down, they don't need electricity, they don't overheat and they're a great addition to your lighting kit.

### Single-point Lighting

For many amateur productions this is going to be the "norm" situation – simply using one light to lift the gloom and illuminate the subject/subjects. However, do not be fooled into thinking there is not any flexibility in this scenario because there is.

It has often been suggested that an ideal starting point for this system is for us to imagine where the light in the scene is coming from. Depending on what you are shooting, try and establish from where natural or artificial light would shine onto your subject. You have options here: it could come from above, or to the side of the subject, or it could even come from directly in front of them. What you have to decide is whether the shadows cast by the light look right or wrong. Study your subject, if you have

a monitor hooked up, look at it. Do you want the shadows to appear where they are? Feel free to move the light around, and if you have the capability, vary the beam to give less harsh shadows.

In lighting design the terms **hard light** and **soft light** are used to make the distinction between different types of shadow. If you can think that sunshine provides a harsh, abrasive light with very defined shadows, while a cloudy sky will provide shadows which are softer and more diffused. Decide which of the two suits your video the best and implement that one.

### Two-point Lighting

With a second lamp in your set-up you do not have to pay as much attention to the harsh shadows that might be created by a single-point shoot. Your first light can now be positioned to provide a hard light, or as it is now referred to, your **key light** and is adding both shape and texture. This new second light is known as a **fill light** and is now providing a softer tone to the scene.

With the key light only, the camcorder will not be able to make out any detail from the shaded parts of our scene, but once we have added the fill light, these areas will become illuminated. However, because fill light is soft light, we will not be contradicting the shadow thrown by the key light.

Although lighting has very few set rules, and precious little right or wrong approaches – this is art we are talking about here, if it works for you, then it is the right thing to do – it is generally accepted that a fill light will be placed on the opposite side to the key light.

### Three-point Lighting

Making your lighting set-up a trio, means finding another name for this new light, and that is **back light**. It is placed behind the subject, and shines towards the camcorder, in order that your subject stands out from the background. This is especially important if your subject is wearing dark colours against a dark background, as camcorders do not distinguish between shades of black!

It is possible to use either a hard or soft light, as a backlight as you should not see the shadows it creates.

Figs 43–44 – Two examples of single-point lighting with the main light source coming from a different angle, one behind the camera, and one to the left.

Fig 45 – Two-point lighting: This will achieve a natural look.

Fig 46 – Three-point lighting.

Figs 47–48 – Placing your main light source at different heights reduces or increases the length of shadows.

## Accessories

In their professional capacity, a lighting cameraman/woman will have a massive bag of tricks for subtly shading and emphasizing light. With all the accessories and apparel a videomaker already has, it is unlikely you will be able to match them. However, it is worth knowing a few bits and pieces.

*Barn Doors:* A frame of four metal flaps which fit around a light, barn doors can be fitted to spotlights or floodlights to restrict the beam size.

*Gels and Filters:* Just like digital camcorders, lights can use filters to change their colour. There is a wide range of coloured gels, as they are called, which come in rolls and are cut to fit into a frame that slots in front of the light. It is possible to get them in solid colours, or for more subtle shading and texture, pastel and graduated gels are available.

*Scrims:* A scrim is a screen placed in front of the light to reduce its intensity, but without altering its colour temperature.

*Fig 49 – Barn doors around a light make its beam more directional.*

*Snoots:* These are like barn doors, only conical in shape rather than square. Snoots are only usually fitted to spotlights so that they can restrict the diameter of the beam. Snoots are available in a range of sizes, and allow the user to shine small circles of light toward a subject in order to highlight certain areas.

*Fig 50 – Learn a few basic rules about light and shadow, and you will be able to achieve the desired result whatever the scene you are shooting.*

PRODUCT

# PRODUCTION TIME

# PRODUCTION TIME

**A**sk any television or production company what digital technology has done for them and you will get a mixed response. While digital video has liberated videomakers to a point where the number of people needed to make a production can sometimes be just one, naturally this has caused "downsizing" within the media industry. News crews reporting on location can often consist of a cameraman and a reporter, or in some cases just a reporter who operates the camera by remote.

## PUTTING A CREW TOGETHER

For videomakers this set of circumstances shows the power of digital videomaking over its analogue past, as it has reduced the division between "them and us", between the professionals and the amateurs. Digital video has also redefined the term broadcast quality. Having an entire production crew milling around a location – especially where documentaries and reality TV shows are concerned – often diminishes the responses of the protagonists. In fact, it is possible to record people even with the smallest digital camcorders without them registering that they are being recorded (although the associated legal difficulties are multiplying). Digital video is good enough to be seen on television (and increasingly cinema) screens, and now what matters most is the content and the context of the programme.

The image and sound quality of DV is as high as its ease-of-use factor. And, with the affordability of computer-based editing it is possible to complete the picture by cutting your video, and then distributing it on digital video tape, VHS, DVD, Video CD or via the internet.

Not surprisingly, this has caused numerous videomakers to turn into one-man bands, working on their own to produce a variety of video content. However, to think that you have to work "on your todd" as a digital videomaker is missing both the point and the benefit of working with a crew. As we have already mentioned, context is everything and, if you are planning to shoot any complicated production, such as a fiction film (heck, even if you are shooting a wedding) then it is very reassuring to know that you have someone checking that you are actually recording the sound while you are concentrating on the visuals. However, crew

*Fig 1 – The boom in reality television is due, at least in part, to the quality of modern digital video camcorders.*

*Fig 2 – It helps to ensure that all you need is in place before you start to shoot a scene.*

members can also be a contradiction, so remember that while it is helpful to have extra eyes, ears and hands, it is also other people to manage... and feed! Try to tailor the number of crew you need to the scale of the production. Crew members do not have to do just one job.

## You're the Boss

Since you are the one reading this book, we are going to assume that you are the head honcho, top banana, so to speak, and it is your little baby we are filming. You become the director and, unless you really want someone else to do the lens work, you are the camera operator as well. It is easy to get caught up with just the images, so you want a member of crew to look after sound. OK, meet your sound recordist. It is their job to monitor the sound levels, to check that the sound is not booming away from the microphone and distorting the audio. They need to ensure that dialogue is recorded cleanly, because it is unlikely on an amateur production that you will get a shot at dialogue replacement –

even with the sophistication of computer editing. You can simply allocate the sound recordist a set of headphones, plug them into the camcorder, and ask them to check the sound, or you can double up, and, if you are using a microphone on a boom, ask them to hold the boom. This ensures they are more involved and can actually have an effect on the sound being laid down.

Next up, and getting a little more professional here, we have the lighting technician (or assistant). As you might have seen in the previous chapter, lighting can be a complicated business and a lighting tech can lift that burden from you. They will be in charge of positioning the lights as well as suggesting what gels it might be useful to use. A lighting tech also has a responsibility for safety. Lights can get very, very hot, and also have an alarming tendency to explode, and no inexperienced crew members should be allowed to move or touch them without the lighting tech's say-so.

Continuity might sound like a luxury from a film set, but it is a useful function and if performed

Fig 3 – Being a crew member involves a lot of standing around! But you need to be ready to go when the director needs you.

Fig 4 – Rewards for a good job, well done, can come in many forms.

**Crew Checklist**
Meet your crew, and find out what they do!

• *Producer:* Often "The Big Cheese" but, more appropriately on low-budget productions, finds cash, actors, food, equipment and solves problems.

• *Director:* Shouts "Action!", bosses everyone about. But remember, it is their vision you are recreating.

• *Camcorder Operator:* Helps set up shots, tells Director if take is a good one, provides vision.

• *Sound Recordist/Monitor:* Checks sound levels and quality of recorded sound, wears headphones, can be deafened very easily.

• *Lighting Assistant:* Helps create mood of video with lighting design, turns on and positions lights!

• *Continuity:* checks If you are crossing the line, ensures actors are wearing the right apparel and speaking the right lines, location is free from period clashes, takes photos.

• *Production Assistant:* Real title = gopher. Gets tape, batteries and tea, on occasion gets to hold clapperboard.

• *Effects:* If your project involves special effects, somebody will need to set them up. If those effects are to be added later in post-production, it's helpful to have someone there making sure you get the right shots to make those effects possible.

correctly it can save you having to re-shoot scenes, or entire sequences. Essentially, continuity ensures an actor is wearing the correct clothes for each shot, that their hairstyle has not changed, that their make-up remains consistent and that the cigarette they are smoking in the scene does not get longer and shorter as you do new takes or shots! With so much going on it is easy to forget that your lead actor was wearing jeans in the scene you shot yesterday, but today is wearing suit trousers. The two scenes, shot on separate days, can easily be meant to be next to each other in your edit. Little things like cigarettes, or the eating of food might cause nightmares in post-production as you spot the differences in scenes. Continuity should also check the actors are speaking the right parts of dialogue and can prevent you from "crossing the line" by shooting a sequence from the wrong side.

For some of your crew you will have to be creative in supplying titles. Production Assistant sounds so much more professional than gopher, though essentially that is what this role is. You might want them to use the clapperboard –they will like that – but they are also useful for supplying sustenance. Having a crew means having to feed people, and good work does not often come from a malnourished crew. You will probably be working long hours and you want everyone with you, not against you.

For the bigger, and finer, things in life you might want to employ a Producer. Although in most low-budget DV productions the "videomaker" would probably take this role, if you can find someone to produce, it can free the "artist" in you to concentrate purely on the creative side. A Producer ensures budgets are met, assuming that there is a budget to start with. They can liaise with other crew members and can diffuse tricky situations, can smooth the use of a location with "the authorities" whilst also being on hand at a later date to take some of the credit for your successful production!

**PLAN AHEAD**
Embarking on a shoot is a risky business. It is the point in your production when you become irrevocably committed to spending serious money and time on your video, and you do not want things to start going wrong. You need to have dealt with every possible problem before going on a shoot, because once you are kitted up and on location, or in a studio, you are spending money every second you are there and do not want to be wasting time on anything that is not vital.

Sorting out a checklist before starting the shoot is the best way of avoiding time-consuming

*Fig 5 – Being prepared for the filming location is vital.*

that they are expected to provide batteries, tapes, DATs etc, albeit at your expense. Production assistants or runners should be dealing with the elements of the shoot that are there to keep people happy and safe, as opposed to ending up on screen: food, first aid kits, etc.

Before you delegate anything, however, you need to be aware of what tasks

mistakes, and it also helps you decide which people you can delegate jobs to. Equipment, for example, should be the priority of its respective departments. Camera operators and sound crews should know

and requirements you have, as well as working out things that are necessary for the shoot. Below is a selection of common pitfalls and handy hints that will help things go smoothly.

*Fig 6 – Shooting on location is great, but make sure you are safe, legal and well prepared.*

Make sure you have permission to shoot in your particular locations and make sure it is not just permission from some chap who happened to be passing through at the time. If you are shooting at a factory, for example, it may not be enough simply to have permission from the owner. The shift manager may have concerns about the potential workflow disruption you may cause; the security staff may be worried about having so many strangers on site; the health and safety officer may not be keen on having cables gaffer-taped all over the place. All these people can throw a perfectly justifiable spanner in the works. If you cannot get in touch with all of them, at least make sure that whoever you have spoken to has checked things with them and get copies of your permission in writing to prove you are allowed to shoot where you say you are.

When doing your *reconnoitre* do not just be thinking about the actual composition of your shots – make sure you keep an eye out for practical details as well. Are the power points conveniently located and suitable for your equipment or will you be running cables all over the place? If so, take gaffer tape to secure cables to the floor. (In fact, take gaffer tape everywhere, it is incredibly useful stuff.) Is there any annoying background noise that will mess up your soundtrack? Are certain areas particularly busy and likely to pose continuity problems? Forewarned is forearmed.

Think about your shooting ratio and adjust it according to specific situations. There is no point planning a 6:1 ratio (six minutes of shooting for every minute that reaches the screen) for easily controllable studio shots, and you definitely do not want to allow yourself a 3:1 ratio for a location shoot where any number of unscheduled occurrences can take you over the number of tapes you had planned to shoot. This is a digital video. It's cheap, so burn tape as much as you like when in the field and make up for any extravagances by being more conservative with your safer shots – inserts, studio shoots, etc.

*Figs 7–10 – Stately homes and railway stations will have safety and security concerns, and you should show consideration whenever you are shooting in public.*

*Fig 11 – A set-up diagram will help you plan your camera moves before any tape is wasted.*

Plan your shots and set-ups carefully. Never be chronological with your shooting order and set-ups unless that is the most practical method, which it rarely is.

If Scene One is in a dining room, Scene Two in a bedroom and Scene Three back in the dining room, then film Scenes One and Three back-to-back before moving all your kit. Similarly, if a scene is composed of several shots from different angles, take the similarly angled shots back-to-back rather than constantly lugging tripods and camcorders backwards and forwards across the set.

Draw a storyboard from your script that shows the action as it will be onscreen, then draw a bird's eye diagram of each set or location and mark out where you will need to set up to get the shots on your storyboard. Then go through the script, with the diagram to hand, noting scene and shot numbers next to their respective shot locations until you have clusters of numbers scattered around your diagram. This way you can break the whole thing down into fewer repeated set-ups and also check to make sure you will not be crossing the line with certain shots.

If you are doing this, you will find that the contents of your DV tapes are hopelessly garbled and in totally the wrong order, but that is OK – clapperboards are for more than just synchronizing sound. If you are recording a separate, off camera soundtrack (and we hope you are – it gives much better results) then you will already have a clapperboard that will allow you to sync the audio from mini disc or DAT to the video. On this clapper board, log the scene, shot and take number and when it comes to editing time, you will find that your non-sequential recordings are no more inconvenient to work with than those shot in linear fashion.

Having worked out your shot list, move on to a call list. If you are shooting Scenes 2, 8 and 15, for example, at a certain location on a certain day, then make sure everyone who needs to be there will be there and no one who need not be there ends up wasting a day on site. List the scenes, the locations and addresses, the cast and crew members required to be there, the equipment needed (there is no point dragging several metres of dolly track to a location that will only feature in static shots), etc. Distribute this list to all cast and crew and make sure they know when and where they are supposed to be and how to get there. Add an appendix to this list showing alternate locations for certain days in case it rains at one of your external locations and you want to avoid downtime by substituting an alternative.

When timetabling your shoot, consult with those in the know. If your gaffer says it will take two hours to set up the lights for a specific shot then there is no point planning to finish that shot and move on in one hour. Remember to schedule in a little leeway for errors, consultations, discussions and such-like (but not too much leeway – you have to stay in control of the time and money being spent on the shoot). A good rule of thumb is that everything will take twice as long as you think it will and however much time you allow, there will still be things you wished you'd done later on.

Another thing to allow for in the schedule are last-minute onset rehearsals, be it for nervous interview subjects or amnesiac actors. Again, be careful how much time you allow. An over rehearsed interview subject will come across as being too practised and boring, and an actor can lose the vibrant edge of their performance if they have been through it too many times. Equally, do not be too stingy with rehearsal times – no one should have to appear on camera if they feel totally uncomfortable doing so. It is a question of getting to know your people and figuring out when they need the practice and when they are just nervously procrastinating.

Remember to allocate time for lunch. Most of your cast and crew are probably working cheap or for free and it is not a lot to ask that they at least be fed. Even if your budget is too tight to run to on-site catering, make (or get the runner to make) a couple of big flasks of tea and coffee and a selection of sandwiches and snacks.

Lastly, bring cash and cheque books. You may think you have everything you need, but you never know when you will need to improvise. On one shoot, several years ago, we had the embarrassing experience of having to use all our petty cash to bribe away local urchins – too young to be given a fat lip, but old enough to carry out their threats of pinching a few cameras. The only solution, in this particular case, was bribery, which worked a treat.

We are not suggesting that you specifically budget for backhanders, but it illustrates the point that you never know precisely what might crop up during a shoot.

Remember, no plan survives first contact with the enemy. This is not a reason not to plan. It simply means that a good shoot is as much about how creatively you deal with your plan's failure as it is about how well your plan was constructed. Your production can often be improved rather than compromised when things go wrong because it forces you to think on your feet and knowing you've got everything else under control will allow you to do that. Your plans are the safety net that allow you to perform more adventurous stunts.

*Fig 12 – Using storyboarding lets you plan your images in advance.*

:SHOOTIN

# SHOOTING SITUATIONS

# SHOOTING SITUATIONS

::SHOOTING SITUATIONS::

There are a million reasons why you'll find yourself pressing the big red record button but of those, the main situations are likely to be: fiction, documentary, interviews, weddings and holidays. Many of the same shooting principles apply to these scenarios but there are techniques within each discipline which are useful to know.

Everyone armed with a camcorder can make holiday videos, because it's the easiest form of videomaking – virtually everyone takes at least one holiday a year and it ostensibly requires you just to point and shoot – to record your holiday memories. However, if you want to get the best out of digital video then every time you press the record button you need to have thought about what and how you are shooting. Even if you just want to make a record of your holiday, giving some consideration to the images you take will ensure you have a video more than one or two of you will want to watch!

## FICTION FINDING

We thought we'd start with the most ambitious project videomakers can tackle – the fiction video. This can be in short form (under 15–20 minutes) or a full-on feature-length production, but the same basic rules apply.

You might ask, "Why would I want to make a fiction video? Surely my digital camcorder's just an amateur machine capable of recording the odd event?" They are good questions. The answer is that the domestic camcorder and computer are now capable of shooting and editing films at the same technical quality as is used on television, and in the case of High Definition, camcorders almost at the quality of cinema film.

By dealing in fiction you are doing something different and having to think about video in a multitude of ways. It will involve working with actors, directing action, working with a script – and perhaps best of all means you can shout "Action!" and mean it.

## Getting Prepared

If you decide to embark on shooting a fiction video you will need to be organized. So where to start? Well as we've looked at scripting and storyboards in previous chapters we'll head there first. Before you shoot a single sequence you need to have an idea, and then you need to have a story. You then need to map out what you need to shoot this story, in terms of equipment, crew and actors. It's simply no use starting a project without a list of everything you are going to use.

**Questions you need to ask are:**

- *Do I need more than one camcorder?* A second camcorder gives you options for recording the same scene from different angles which might be useful when editing. Also consider what accessories you will need: tripod, microphone, headphones, tapes, batteries, charger, rainjacket/camcorder protection?

- *How many crew members do I need, and where can I get them?*

*Fig 1 – Holidays are often the first shooting situation you will find yourself in.*

- *Do I want trained actors or will my friends do it for a laugh?* Tricky one this as your friends might not be able to act, might not be capable of meeting your demands, and might not be your friends after the shoot!

- *Will I need lighting?* If you do then what sort: on camera, handheld or stand-mounted?

- *Which locations will I be using?* And have I actually got permission to film there?

- *What costumes and props do I need?* Where will I get them, and, if this is a period piece what do I need to remember to remove from view? Digital watches, television aerials, cars and planes were not that evident in Victorian Britain!

- *How will I shoot any action sequences I want?* And who will be doing the stunts?

- *What about post-production?* How are you going to edit your film? Does it need effects, 3D animation or compositing and how are they going to be achieved? How will you produce incidental music, titling and sound effects?

- *Where is my film headed?* Are you aiming for YouTube, film festivals, television, video or cinematic release? Knowing the market for your movie will make a world of difference to the way you write, shoot, budget and edit your film. It'll also have a massive impact on the production values you employ (in other words, will you take an hour to shoot a scene or a week and will you shoot it in your living room or have a set built?).

Answering these questions will give you an insight into how complicated (or not) your production is going to be.

*Fig 2 – Using more than one camcorder will help you to cover action scenes comprehensively, as in 1955's* Rebel Without a Cause.

### Don't Lose the Plot

Once you've assembled your equipment, script and actors it's best to embark on a period of rehearsal. Doing this enables the actors to familiarize themselves with the character they are playing. Hopefully they will have done some research into how they (or you) want them to play the role, but you could also ask them to think of a "back story" for the person they are playing. This is information not in the script, and not necessarily relating to the story, but it enables the actors to understand where their character comes from, and *why* they react the way they do to certain situations. It can include where they come from, what their family background is, what jobs they have done and what relationships they have had. A useful tool here is improvisation. Take away their scripts, give them a situation, and ask them to simply "be" their characters in that situation. It will force them to think on their feet and their understanding of their character will grow. In acting terms this is often known as the method approach, and while many actors simply want to turn up and say their lines, it's useful encouraging them to think just a little about the person they are playing.

Rehearsal also helps actors familiarize themselves with their lines. This might seem a little trite, but it's surprising how many performers turn up on location barely on nodding terms with what they are supposed to say. If you choose to use your friends in your video then this might easily be the case. There is a way around the problem of not knowing your lines – and no we don't mean firing the actor – it's known as an idiot board. You simply write down the lines in big text on a piece of card and have someone hold the card out of sight of the camcorder but close enough for the actors to refer to!

The low cost of digital media, and the unobtrusive design of digital camcorders should also allow you to record the rehearsals. This will give you an opportunity to see if the dialogue that's been written works, and sounds realistic, when spoken. It also gives videomakers the opportunity to block out sequence, such as where an actor stands and then moves to within a scene, along with giving the videomaker a chance to try out different shot angles. Just don't let the act of recording distract you from your primary job – directing and shaping the actors' performances.

With rehearsal over, and any adjustments to the scripts and storyboards made, it's time to move to the "in production" stage of your video. You should have a shot list ready along with your shooting schedule. You should have checked the actors and crew can make the times you've stipulated. Try to ensure you don't have to zip back and forth between locations, shooting scenes out of sequence but which need to be shot in the same location, and try to be realistic about how many scenes and how much footage you can shoot each day. Professional productions often have very

*Fig 3 – Professional touches, such as using a clapperboard and numbering your scenes and takes, will help in post-production.*

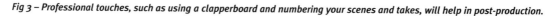

*Fig 4 – Rehearsing scenes shows you what does and does not work.*

long shooting days, often from 5.00 am to after 9.00 or 10.00 pm, but if you are not paying your crew or actors, or even if you're using your friends, try not to subject them to Kubrick and Hitchcockesque demands. Get to a location early and, along with your crew, set up so that everything is prepared before the actors arrive. Check sound levels, light levels and make sure you're not getting in anybody's way, and most important of all, definitely, most absolutely, make sure everyone involved in the production gets some food.

## Recording Contract

One of the real secrets to success in making a fiction video is to think ahead. When you're shooting you should also be thinking about editing. So, don't just yell, "Action!" and start recording – take a few tips from the professionals. It will mean recording more footage than you'll use but will cut down the amount of time spent in the edit, while also ensuring you don't go prematurely grey or lose your hair! In film production, cameras take time to come up to speed, starting the action before the camera achieves "speed" could mean you don't get the shot you want.

This is a good policy to adopt. Start the camcorder recording, the director shouts "Rolling!", get the clapperboard holder to mark the scene (calling out, "Scene one, Take one," etc), then shout, "Action!", have someone count down – five, four, three, two, one – using their fingers to indicate to the actors. Five to three should be spoken as well, to give the sound recordist an idea of sound levels, while two and one should be silent and indicated by fingers only. Each scene should be allowed to overrun for around five seconds before the Director calls, "Cut!" Using this checklist you not only know what scene and take you've recorded and are looking at when in the edit, but also you provide correct sound levels and give the actors the opportunity to do something unexpected at the end of a scene, that you might want to keep.

At the end of a day's shooting try to look at what you've recorded. In film speak these are known as rushes. Digital video has an advantage over film here, in that film has to be processed before the rushes can be viewed, but digital video footage can be viewed immediately. If you want, a scene can be checked as soon as it has been recorded.

*Fig 5 – Fight scenes need to be choreographed to look realistic and to protect your cast.*

## Action Stations

Finally it's worth mentioning action sequences. Even the most pedestrian of stories will require action at some point. It could just be a character running down the street, or falling to the ground after a punch-up. Be wary of anything that could go wrong and injure the actor, the crew or anybody on or near the location. This is especially pertinent if you've adopted the guerilla video-making tactic of not gaining permission to shoot on location, and simply turn up

If you can, it's worth taking a monitor along to the shoot (i.e. a TV screen connected to the camcorder's output).

That way you can watch your footage on a full size TV screen as you record it, and you'll be able to spot bad lighting, poor focus and even the subtleties of the actors' performances live.

and try to get everything on tape before you're moved on. Imagine you decide to get some shots of a character running down London's Oxford Street. The number of people affected by your presence could run into thousands. Be careful. You could even just be shooting a sequence in a quiet park, yet you can still intrude on the public. Also, be aware that if you get passers-by, private

*Figs 6–7 – Action scenes are the centrepiece of many movies, but they can seriously damage the budget if something goes badly wrong.*

buildings, logos, trademarks or copyrighted artworks (including advertising) in shot, you may be open to legal action if you use the footage. And anyone showing the film may ask for evidence that you have permission for the contents of every shot. Always carry a bundle of release forms (you can find them on the internet) around with you so you can keep your production legal.

Action sequences serve several purposes, they make your video more dramatic, increase its tension, atmosphere and pace. The secret here is coverage. In a film or video events don't have to take place in real time – a 10-minute race doesn't need 10 minutes on screen. A mixture of shots will serve your purpose better and make it easier for you to edit a sequence together. Change camera positions regularly, and make sure each shot is significantly different to the previous one. A good tip is to change shot size, starting with a master shot to establish the situation and then move from mid range shots to close-ups and occasionally back to a master shot so the viewer doesn't lose track of what is going on.

Professional productions will employ a stunt man or stunt team to carry out the complicated action sequences, but it's unlikely a low budget amateur production will be able to afford their services. The safety of your entire crew should be paramount so any action sequences should be well choreographed and rehearsed. Again, the range of camera angles can provide the dynamics for you.

Car chases are going to be pretty much out of the question on low budget videos because of the danger involved, but they are possible if you have permission to film in deserted locations well away from main roads and thoroughfares. Accessories manufacturers have a selection of car clamps and suction mounts that will allow you to fasten your (very expensive) digital camcorder to a vehicle, allowing you to get fast moving action, as well as close-ups and interior shots.

It's worth considering getting insurance. Many locations will be happy to let you shoot as long as you're insured, but may ban you if you aren't. Getting insurance can be the cheapest way of providing reassurance to those in charge of potential locations that you're not going to cause trouble.

## Digital Effects

Let's start by dismissing the idea that digital effects are restricted to sci-fi blockbusters. Nowadays most stunt sequences have an element of digital post-

*Fig 8 – Get permission before shooting in busy locations. Tom Cruise and director Cameron Crowe needed to for* Vanilla Sky *(2001).*

production (to make them cheaper, more effective and safer) and almost every film you see has some kind of digital visual effects work involved in it.

Every effects shot has to be carefully planned and you need to know exactly what you're going to do in advance. Just saying "we'll fix that in post-production" will make your edit long, difficult and potentially unsatisfactory.

Here are some of the most commonly used effects in modern films along with a quick outline of the kind of software and skills you'll need to make them work.

**Colour correction** This is used in every film you see and can be done using virtually any editing software. Colour correction allows you to take each shot and alter the colours, brightness and contrast within it. With colour correction you can give an image a whole new atmosphere turning a bright sunny day into a cold dark one, producing harsh high-contrast lighting (as seen in the film *300*) or simply matching the tones of shots from the same scene taken on different days.

**Matte painting** Simply superimposing a painted, photographed or 3D-generated object (often called an overlay) into a shot. Often used to add, for example, a new building to a landscape or to replace a sign or billboard on a building. If you have a still image editing program and a video editor, you can do this, but you'd better not move the camera or things will get a lot more difficult.

**Object removal** Used to paint out wires and devices used to make stunt scenes work, to remove TV aerials from period dramas, to take out unwanted background objects or blur out people or objects you don't have permission to show. This work needs to be done by hand frame by frame, and a second of footage can take hours so keep it to a minimum. Often done using a still image editor like PhotoShop.

**Blue-screen** Shooting an object against a flat single coloured screen means you can replace that screen with another video clip in all but the cheapest video editing packages. It's a well known technique used in every effects movie or news broadcast. To get a good "key" you need to light your backdrop evenly, keep the camera rock steady and make sure your actors aren't wearing the same colour as your screen.

**CGI (Computer-generated-imagery)** Computers are now used to produce realistic backgrounds for sets, cars for car chases, animated characters and creatures, and even people. If you have the skills to produce CGI and the software (3DSmax, Maya, z-brush and Poser are common examples) you can do pretty much anything. However, the quality of the work always depends on the time that can be devoted to it, so plan your shots to make the best of your animation and don't be over-ambitious.

**Compositing** This is the process of adding elements from more than one shot. This can mean superimposing people into previously shot backgrounds, adding CGI to a scene, or adding together parts of a shot filmed separately. For example, a man diving out of the way of a speeding car would be dangerous to shoot. However, shoot the car, then the man without moving the camera, and you can composite the two together. This is generally done with specialist software such as After Effects or Combustion. You need to shoot very specific shots to get this right, and often you need to film an empty frame as well to provide the background.

## INTERVIEWS

In the commercial world, the interview is probably the most common set-up a jobbing camera operator is likely to experience. It doesn't matter if it's a current affairs show, documentary for broadcast, an image film, or product demo. The chances are that somewhere you'll have a talking head. As an amateur, an interview can convey information "straight from the horse's mouth", and is sometimes the only way to explain a subject without resorting to expensive travel, graphics or stock footage. Interviews fall into two categories, single camera and multi-camera shoots.

Let's start with the most basic, single camera interview. It is possible to conduct the interview, operate the camera and adjust the sound all at the same time, but something will be lacking. I guarantee it. Either the technical side will be less than perfect or the subject will notice that they're not getting your full and undivided attention and will not perform their best in front of the camera. Make no mistake,

*Fig 9 – An example of the "over-the-shoulder 2 shot".*

what you're doing here is recording a performance, albeit an unscripted one and your "talent" needs as much attention as the most demanding actor. If you're the director then sit down in position and talk to the interviewee whilst the camera operator sets the lights and the sound recordist fumbles with cables and microphones. If you're the camera person then give the interviewee a warning before zapping them with 800 watts of light. Oh and don't say "I'm going to switch this light on", as you turn on the juice because it's guaranteed that phrase will get the talent looking straight at the unit and consequently blinded for the next five minutes! A good phrase is "Cover your eyes... light coming on."

Decide early on whether the interviewer's questions are going to be part of the programme. If they are, you'll need to have them on-mic. And you might want them in shot. If they're not, you'll need to be able to cut them out – which means making sure the interviewee speaks in complete sentences which include the subject of the question (i.e. never says "yes" or "no") and never having the interviewer interrupt or talk over them.

**Single Life**
For the majority of single camera interviews, a lighting set-up known as "standard portrait" or three-point lighting will provide more than satisfactory results. It's the basis of just about every lighting occasion and once you know how to set it, you can start adjusting and playing with it, expanding your possibilities, secure in the knowledge that if it all goes pear shaped you can quickly bung up a portrait rig without any problem.

If you've got a light meter then use it! Especially in studio or indoor situations where you've got to balance different sources. You might be able to see the features of someone sitting in front of a window and your viewfinder might even seem to show that it's within acceptable limits but beware. The viewfinder shows what the camera chip sees, not

*Fig 10 – The "standard portrait" lighting set-up is the basis of nearly every situation.*

*Fig 11 – Two cameras are useful when the interviewer and interviewee are of different heights.*

what levels the tape records and there can be quite a difference between the two. A good light meter will dispel any doubts you might have and make you look like you really know what you're doing. Turn on the zebra function and levels indicators if your camcorder has them and they will immediately show up any problems with the exposure.

A couple of hints about interviews. Firstly, always make sure that the camcorder can see both of the "victim's" eyes. Profiles tend to lack intimacy and give the impression that the subject is talking to someone who is way off on the sidelines. If the interviewee keeps turning away from the camera then get the reporter close (and I mean close) to the lens axis.

The other annoyance is an interviewee who keeps looking at the camera. This is easily sorted by placing a "reporter light" on top of the camera lens such that it blinds the subject if he looks at it. Cruel, I know, but at least it stops them looking down the tube.

Wherever possible have the camera lens on the same level as the subject's eyes. Place the camera above their eye level and they tend to look weak and

vulnerable, below their eye level implies arrogance and dominance. Some subjects have deep set eyes or heavy eyebrows which throw a shadow onto the eyeballs. Eyes which don't have any highlights or reflections look "dead" and need a bit of help to bring them to life. We've mentioned using an on-camera light to stop subjects looking at the lens, well this is also the cure for pothole eyes. Sometimes the talent will have greasy skin, sweat slightly or simply have the sort of complexion which bounces light like a bowling ball. There are two solutions, one involves small, barely noticeable adjustments to the lights. The other way is to buy a powder compact. A bit of powder on a sweaty brow saves ages messing around with lights and reflectors.

There's a broadcasting mantra which goes "Zoom during the question, not the answer" which is worthy of noting. Like all advice, it's not written in stone and a slow zoom in during a long answer can look really good, especially if the zoom creeps in with a barely perceptible movement. Don't overuse this effect though. Save it for a poignant answer. If it doesn't fit, then save it for another occasion.

The most easily forgotten essential in shooting an interview is the cut-away. You're not going to use all of your interview, so you're going to need to cut. Each time you do that, there will be a jump in the picture (unless the camera angle is radically different for each answer). You need to cover that jump with another shot. This can be a shot of the interviewer (recorded afterwards and often termed "noddies" because it's a shot of the interviewer looking interested and nodding), a close-up of the interviewee's hands or eyes, a shot of whatever they're talking about or relevant images which add colour to the interview, clarify points or describe the interviewee's personality. Get plenty of them because you will definitely regret it in the edit if you don't.

## Trick and Treat

You can "trick" a single camera set-up into a multi-camera shoot by recording the reporter's questions separately and then adding them in the editing. It's best to record these after the interview because (a) the reporter knows the questions he or she has actually asked; and (b) the interviewee is already on tape and can't prepare or rehearse answers.

At this stage the main errors to avoid are: the reporter looking in the same direction as the interviewee, and the eyelines conflicting. If the subject is recorded looking towards frame left, then the questioner should look frame right (and vice versa). Be careful with this technique, it can very easily go wrong and look awful and obviously fake.

Occasionally you'll be asked to record an interview or meeting with more than one camera. This is the sort of challenge which videomakers should be searching high and low for. It's a great opportunity to put a team together and attempt a more complex job. Allow plenty of time to prepare the location and light the set. The same portrait lighting can be deployed on each subject and, with a bit of thought, some lights can be used for more than one purpose. If you're recording a discussion on a stage or hall with a public present, be aware that if you want shots of the public, you'll need to light them as well, without blinding them such that

*Fig 12 – Holidays are, without doubt, the most popular videos shot by camcorder owners.*

*Figs 13–14 – Make holiday videos more visually interesting by looking for some striking images.*

they can't see those taking part!

When directing a multi-camera interview try to get the cameras to vary their shots between close-ups, mid shots and long shots with the emphasis on the close-ups. Also try to make use of the "over-the-shoulder-2-shot" to show both the subjects in relationship to each other. If you are using more than two cameras, then it's a good policy to keep one camera just for the presenter so that you've always got a shot you can cut to.

If you're making a documentary in which there are several interviews cut together, try to make sure some are facing left to right and some right to left.

Finally, when you are editing, follow your feelings rather than the rules. If the cut looks and feels wrong, it is wrong. It's what's being said that matters, not how beautifully it's filmed, so be prepared to break any of the rules if your interviewee is saying something important. Try to avoid cutting long shot to long shot and – whatever you do – maintain a sense of humour. Multi-camera jobs are all about teamwork and co-operation.

## HOLIDAYS

Without doubt the most common use for a camcorder, aside from "home movies" (we're not being tasteless it's actually true) is to record a document of your annual holiday. Now there is one big problem associated with this, and we're sure almost everyone has experienced it. The daunting invite to just pop round and see a friend's holiday video has seen the

*Fig 15 – Sand and salt water damage camcorders. Be protected from the elements.*

demise of more than a few friendships! Sitting through a couple of hours of badly shot, boring holiday video is more than any reasonable person should have to bear, and what's so frustrating is that it doesn't have to be this way.

The ideal holiday video should be a taster, illustrating the outstanding moments from what was a relaxing or invigorating trip. Every shot has to earn its right in your production and only then will you be able to invite the neighbours round.

## Two Tribes

There are two distinct approaches to shooting a holiday video. One is a relaxed, care-free style, grabbing a few choice images but not taking your camcorder everywhere. The second is a full on, "this is a trip of a lifetime, not to be missed, pack everything" approach. And which one you pick depends on the trip you take.

*Fig 16 – The camcorder can bring back holiday memories more vividly than photos.*

You can, unquestionably, bring back a decent holiday record by just taking your camcorder and the odd accessory with you. On the other hand, if you don't view videomaking as a chore, and see it as an integral part of your expedition, then you can choose to take a carefully requisitioned amount of equipment.

Let's start with the first option. Before you travel group together all your equipment and then piece by

*Fig 17 – If filming familiar sights, at least try to look for interesting angles.*

piece discard the stuff you know in your heart of hearts you won't use.

You should be left with a digital camcorder, a couple of tapes, a spare battery, a mains charger (with the appropriate adaptor for the country you're travelling to) and maybe a couple of filters. Two tapes, probably around two hours' worth, should be more than enough raw material for any two-week vacation, because you're going to be shooting wisely. Filters aren't essential, so weigh up the practicalities of taking them. However, a plain skylight filter might be useful as it protects the lens from potential problems such as sand and grit.

So what you're leaving behind is a tripod, because you can use walls, posts, fences, anything as a form of stabilization, headphones – remember it's a holiday video not a film set, and believe us you don't want the unnecessary attention, lights and a microphone. You can do all that you need with the basics and some imagination.

**Be Creative**

Unless something jaw-droppingly exciting is happening, never press the record button until you've thought of an idea. Ideas are the saviour for holiday videomakers – and the poor souls you inflict your video on – as they can transform a dull situation into a truly entertaining spectacle. As you travel to your destination, try to note down some ideas of what you'd really like to capture, and when it's feasible to actually go and video it. A travel guide book is useful here, allowing you to pinpoint tourist attractions and the off-the-beaten-track locations you might want to capture.

Don't start filming as soon as you get to your location, instead spend time getting a feel for your destination. If there's any chance of revisiting the location before your return journey, then go back once you've worked out what to do. Friends and family can go and enjoy a relaxing coffee or unexpected shopping expedition, while you quickly nab the shots you've been pondering over for the last

*Fig 18 – Lens glare is usually to be avoided, but, in the right circumstances, can add texture to your shots.*

couple of days. They'll thank you more for that than for keeping them somewhere longer than necessary, while you dash around hoping you've got enough material.

Not everywhere you venture will have a *laissez-faire* attitude to filming so find out where and when you can film. For example the streets of New York and Los Angeles might seem like a permanent film set but you might be asked by police to stop filming, purely because you don't have a permit. Strange, but true. It's not only foreign outdoor locations that could create filming problems, museums and galleries can have strict anti-video/photography policy, so be careful here as well.

**Short and Sweet**

The most common videomaking mistake, especially on holiday videos, is the length of time each shot lasts. You don't have to stay on the same shot for several minutes to take everything in. The human eye processes information very quickly and your viewers want to be entertained, not bored. Keep shot lengths short, anything more than five or six seconds for a shot, when nobody is talking, is too long. Also be keen to embrace a variety of angles. Don't just put the camcorder to your eye and press record, that way all your shots will invariably be at the same height. Try mixing low and high angle shots, as well as including a variety of long, medium and close-up shots. And remember if you want to be closer to a subject, move closer to it, don't hit that zoom button during recording. You can use the zoom for close-ups, of course, just make sure you do it before you start recording. Ensure you also find the time to shoot some cut-aways to use as fill between shots and sequences. When it comes to editing, cut-aways can be an absolute godsend in covering up mistakes or shots that don't last as long as you want them to.

Travelling light also lets the videomaker make use of the beauty of digital camcorders – their size. Digital camcorders provide an opportunity for unobtrusive filming. You can take them along to most locations and shoot away without the public realizing what you're doing.

**Light and Shade**

If you are on a sun-kissed holiday then there are a couple of situations you should take into consideration. Light is very different all over the world, but wherever you get harsh sunshine your camcorder is not going to like it. If you can move to manual exposure and stop down to reduce the amount of light entering the lens, otherwise you'll have a holiday video that looks more bleached

*Fig 19 – Sunsets can be dramatic subjects and need no explanation.*

*Fig 20 – Holiday videos can be a permanent reminder of a special time.*

than your hair. If you don't have manual exposure try and move to a program AE settings, such as sand and snow specifically designed for bright light, and if you don't have that, then try an AE setting which reduces the exposure to at least some degree. Natural light reflects and this in itself can cause a problem with lens glare, you don't want natural sunlight rebounding into the lens, as it can damage the camcorders lens and circuitry.

Images as beautiful as they might be require a decent soundtrack to complement them, so be sure to think about whether you want to add music or narration at a later date. If you do then you'll have to put the camcorder in its 12-bit PCM stereo mode, so you can audio dub at a later date. If you don't intend to add anything then put the camcorder in its 16-bit PCM stereo mode to ensure the sound you record is the best it can be.

And once you are back home again, please give some serious thought to editing your holiday video. Even if you have been judicious with the amount of footage you've shot, you will still have more than you need (or should have!). Spending some time separating the wheat from the chaff will make for a truly watchable video.

Finally do take a break... it's a holiday after all!

## Excess Baggage

Alright. Well, so much for the easy option, but what about the videomaker who wants everything. Well, you'll be pleased to know that although you'll be taking more equipment the advice is more to the point than option one!

The same rules on shot lengths, angles, permission, exposure, sound and editing still apply but the planning stage is a little more involved. If you have decided to make shooting a video a central theme of your holiday then you first need to decide what to take and you'll also need to decide how you will be transporting your valuable equipment. Along with your camcorder, you'll be stowing away a tripod, headphones, a microphone, maybe a light, extra lenses, filters – essentially all the stuff you've left behind in option one. With all this extra equipment you will need a durable and large holdall or even a camcorder rucksack. There are many on the market, but you might be surprised at quite how expensive they are. Still, compared to the expense of your digital camcorder and all the accessories, the investment is worth it.

Planning is even more important if you're taking this seriously and you should look into gaining permission in advance if you're considering visiting any out of the way,

Figs 21–28 –
Variety is the
key to successful
documentaries.
Different shot
sizes, cut-aways,
using maps, signs,
and a multitude of
settings all help to
create an interesting
atmosphere.

or extreme places. A good tip for creating a fully-rounded holiday video is to capture footage of maps, trails, visitor passes and still photos of the places you've visited, and perhaps music that's indigenous to the region, so that you can incorporate them into your completed production.

Another thing to bear in mind, should you be travelling alone, is not to forget to put yourself in the video from time to time. It's often the case that a videomaker returns from a trip, exhibits their work, only for people to ask where were you then!

## DOCUMENTARIES

There is a richness and diversity to shooting documentaries that can probably only be equalled by the creativity involved in shooting a fiction video. As far as documentaries go, the world is your oyster. You can pick any subject life has to offer and turn it into a short or long form video of note. Fortuitously documentary making offers the videomaker a chance to break away from the constriction of shooting a scripted fiction video, or the formulaic nature of weddings and interviews. This is possible because a lot of the time the videomaker has no control over what happens. Good documentaries come from good observation and a key to this is getting access to situations and making the subjects feel natural and relaxed, rather than trying to dictate what happens and when.

Shot lengths will be much longer in documentary making as you simply have to keep rolling and wait for "life" to happen. This means that editing is the key to success. You will undoubtedly shoot more footage in a short documentary than a short film or interview. It is once you have the footage that you will see how the documentary will develop, and for this reason it's worth being open minded about what direction the video takes. Because you have no pre-ordained shooting script, your initial theme might change, your central character might not be the most interesting aspect of your material in the end, and you might end up disproving any point you had intended to make.

It's not often appreciated that a documentary needs a script as much as a fiction film does. Documentary scripts are generally looser and shorter

*Fig 29–32 – Consider your audio options. Will all your dialogue be written in advance and delivered to camera, or will you add narration later, or will you have a blend of voice-over and interviews?*

Figs 33–36 –
*Mix shot sizes,
but don't cross
the line in a
sequence – as
in the second
image here.*

in that things often happen which fall outside of the planned shoot and which take the programme in a new direction, but it's as essential to know what you're aiming to get on a factual shoot as it is for a fiction shoot. Most documentaries have two scripts. The first is written after the research has been done – detailing roughly what the narrator (if there is one) will say and what you want from the interviewees, and shoots. This gives the initial structure to the piece. The second script is written after the shooting and gives a firm plan to the edit, as well as scripting any voiceover or graphics shots which are needed.

## Access All Areas

As well prepared as you might be for documentary shooting, it's likely that you will run with the bare essentials most of the time: a camcorder, basic microphone and lighting. Audiences don't expect intricate tracking shots or smooth Steadicam work in documentaries, they are increasingly media literate and understand context, and you can take comfort from the fact they won't expect *Lawrence of Arabia* standard cinematography!

The success of fly-on-the-wall and reality TV shows is that they get close to their subjects, warts 'n' all, if you like. And digital video has played an enormous part in achieving this. Digital camcorders are small enough to be unobtrusive, and their image and sound quality is capable of rendering a sound recordist and lighting assistant surplus to requirements most of the time. Imagine this scenario: you are trailing the Managing Director of a small publishing affair as he is implementing potentially unpopular changes on his staff. He is far more likely to be candid with you as you interview him, or video him with staff members, if there is just one person with a digital camcorder. Re-jig the scenario and follow him with a team of three of four people and you'll no doubt see some impressive clamming up.

Again audiences don't expect gloriously lit scenes, or moody and intense situations courtesy of intrepid lighting design. They expect the odd grainy moment, the odd dark corridor, the odd incorrectly white balanced moment – context is everything, and if what you're showing them is entertaining or

*Fig 37 – Weddings and civil partnerships need to be well planned. If you miss your shot, you don't get a second chance.*

fascinating they'll follow you. The same goes for sound – just make sure you pick up what you need, nobody is expecting dynamic stereo switching and sound effects – just the juicy tidbits of gossip!

## Clearance and Ethics

In a documentary, perhaps more than in any other kind of filmmaking, you are putting yourself on the line and putting yourself in a position where you will have to take ethical decisions.

Your film will probably contain some kind of conflict – whether that's the conflict between two people, the points-of-view or ways-of-life of which you are presenting examples, or simply the conflict between the way you're portraying an individual, company, country or organisation and the way they see themselves.

Tensions will run high, and you have responsibilities over and above the responsibility to your film. You have to be fair, even to those whose viewpoint is abhorrent to you; you have to be sensitive when it comes to material which is emotional or graphic and you have to be respectful of the rights of others. Not least because people can and will sue you if you aren't.

At the very least, make sure each interviewee and those responsible for each filming location sign a release form stating that they give you the right to use their words and locations in any way you like.

Of course, there are always exceptions.

Michael Moore doesn't usually get clearance (but he does occasionally get sued). Those filming undercover don't get release forms, but they have to be doubly sure they've got their facts right and they do risk legal action and violence. *Be careful.*

## WEDDINGS AND CIVIL PARTNERSHIPS

Ding dong indeed! Weddings and civil partnerships are fraught, intense, exhausting affairs, and not just for the participants. They are the most traumatic occasions for a videomaker, they do not offer you the chance of a re-shoot, you are at the mercy of the weather, the relevant authorities and all the arrangements that rise above "the video" as a priority on the big day. By relevant authorities, we are talking about the service itself, the venue and the conductor, be it a religious or a civil affair.

You can plan until you're blue in the face, but it's worth nothing, unless you are quick to react on the day. And that is how you succeed at wedding videography – you act and react fast. Still, videoing weddings can be a worthy and fruitful occupation – more than a few serious videomakers use it as a regular earner – and there is a lot of satisfaction in making what could be viewed as a boring situation into a visual spectacle that will bear replaying.

The first rule of Fight Club... sorry... of wedding videos is give the client your best. It's their big day

*Fig 38–41 –
Recce your
location:
check out the
best and least
obstructive
locations for
your camera
and mic,
but most
importantly,
get permission
to film.*

and an important moment for family and friends. Speak to the couple about what sort of video they'd like, and always remember to speak to the relevant authority about permission to video and whether any fee is payable to them. You should also check about copyright for music, as well as performing rights licenses for the choir and organists.

Research your location, think about where you want to place the camcorder(s). And then remember to ask the authority whether it's OK to place your equipment there. For lighting requirements discuss what's feasible – could the church increase the light, or dim it, can you bring any stand-mounted lights in, etc.? You might have to make do with available light, which could alter where you need to place the camcorder.

You really should consider making the production a two-camera shoot. The service can be long (over an

hour) and if you don't want to look at one uninterrupted shot for an hour, you'll need two cameras – one capturing the main action and the other covering the crowd and taking close-ups and reaction shots. Also, there are practical considerations. If you're filming at the bride's house, you'll need to capture her leaving. You'll then need to get to the venue before she does to capture her arrival *and* be at the altar in time to film the groom's reaction as she walks down the aisle. If you have two camera operators, this is a lot easier.

If possible try to rehearse the sound recording, as churches can boom and echo away. Try and get to a rehearsal, if there is one, and make sure you have a selection of microphones to choose from – even if you have to hire them. You might want to record ambient and background sounds on a separate audio only recorder, while using a directional mic, close to the couple (a radio-lapel mic on the groom is a good move) and priest, to pick up the ceremony. A microphone designed to give a general sound recording, such as the one usually built into your DV camcorder, will leave you with variable sound quality and couples are notoriously quiet when speaking their vows.

It's up to the happy couple how in-depth you go with the video – not everyone wants to be videoed getting ready for the big day. But whatever you present them with at the end of the day, make sure it's edited tightly, and compresses some wonderful memories

into a tidy, efficient, watchable package that family and friends won't feel they have to endure rather than enjoy. Titles are a necessity for rounding out the package, and be tasteful with the music soundtrack, should you wish to include any.

If you can, capture brief interviews throughout the day with the friends and families as well as the participants. These can be the highlights of the day – giving guests a chance to send a message to the couple.

With DVD being the distribution method of choice, it's now possible (and good practice) to include two versions – a potted (15 minute) edit of just the significant moments, and a full length version split into chapters (preparations, service, first dance, speeches, etc.) that is available from the DVD menu.

## A WOE-FREE WEDDING
Your location list might go a little something like this:
- Research location
- Speak to relevant authorities and gain permissions where necessary
- Arrive early on wedding day!
- Footage of bride and groom getting ready
- Guests arriving at the venue
- Groom and best man awaiting fate!
- Outside the venue as bride arrives
- Bride enters venue, walks up aisle if in a church
- Ceremony
- Confetti, celebration, depart for reception
- Arrive Reception
- The "line out" – traditionally when the couple meet and greet their guests on the way in to the reception. Deadly dull, but it means that every auntie gets a shot in the video.
- Speeches and toasts
- Cutting of the cake
- First dance
- Evening "Do"
- Interviews

# EDITING

# EDITING

**E**diting is basically storytelling. You start off with shot footage, which, though it may have a vague theme to it, really doesn't say anything particular to the viewer other than "Here's when I turned the camera on and off". It's not a story, it's a sequence of events, and there's a big difference. Anyone who's ever had to sit through an hour of un-edited holiday video will be able to tell you that.

When you're editing, you're not just cutting out the rubbish. It's not about simply removing the badly-shot and overlong scenes or even taking out everything that's not interesting. Good editing often means rejecting some of your best material simply because it doesn't fit in with the story you're trying to tell and this holds true whether you're editing a cinema film, cutting a documentary or making a holiday video.

Michelangelo famously said that he didn't carve a statue – he saw the statue in the marble, and freed it by cutting away everything that wasn't part of it. That's a pretty good analogy for editing but, just as there are an infinite number of statues in a block of marble, there are an infinite number of stories in your raw footage and they're always there throughout the editing process, distracting you from the one you're trying to tell.

If your story is going to have a shape, you need to plan that shape, and that means knowing before you start what story you're trying to tell, how you're going to tell it and, just as importantly, how long the finished work is going to be. If you don't know while you're editing if your story is moments from its climax or if it's just reaching its mid-point, then there's something seriously wrong.

## STORY STRUCTURE

A lot has been written about the process of storytelling. It's not a completely prescriptive process and what makes one story stand out from another is often a matter of personal taste. However there are a few generic storytelling tools you'll find used in most stories – both factual and fictional – that are worth taking note of:

*The set-up* – Most stories start with a set-up that introduces the viewer to the world in which the story will take place, and the characters they're going to be following. In the case of a factual programme, it might be a short introduction, or a set of headlines or clips taken from the show. In the case of fiction, it's often a scene that introduces the main character and gives you an idea of the atmosphere of their world.

*The inciting incident* – Once you've set the scene, you've generally got a couple of minutes to provide

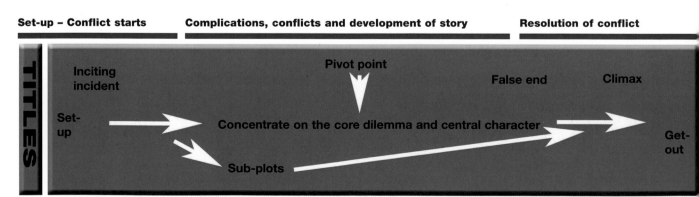

*Fig 1 – A diagram of the basic storytelling structure used by many factual and fictional films.*

the "inciting incident" before viewers start to drift. This is the moment when the challenge or dilemma of your story is introduced. It's the point at which the main question that the programme is intended to pose is put. It grabs the viewer's attention and it makes the rest of the story happen. In a documentary, you'll often get a narrator asking the question directly or boldly putting across a controversial viewpoint. In a fiction film, you might see an action scene (although there's usually an emotional subtext to it) or an emotional moment. Either way, it's the emotional dilemma that will carry the viewer through the movie.

*Sub-plots* – Your inciting incident will get things going. From that moment, the characters (in a fictional film) or the viewer (in a factual one) know that they have a question they *have* to answer or a challenge they *have* to meet. Sub-plots are stories within the central story that fill in colour or complicate the journey. They create more questions and, to a certain extent, distract from the central theme. They're secondary, but they add to the central story, and it's often the sub-plots and complications that define the length of your programme. A Bond film would be pretty useless if Bond went straight for the main villain, never fell in love, played poker or fought henchmen in different parts of the world. Likewise, a documentary which asked the question, "Did Richard III really kill the princes in the tower?", then promptly answered it with a resounding "Yes" and rolled the credits, would be fulfilling its promise, but wouldn't be taking the viewer on a journey they'd remember.

*Pivot point* – Somewhere in the centre of your piece, there's often a point at which the story pivots. It's the "Is it this way or that way?" moment – the point at which we discover something which makes us (and in fiction – the main character) certain what's really going on. From that moment, there's no turning back. We may not know exactly how things are going to end, but we know what has to be done. It's the moment at which you can often hear phrases such as (in fiction) "This time it's personal!" or (in documentary) "But then suddenly something happened that was to change the world forever."

*False end* – You have to keep the audience on their toes. If they know exactly what's going to happen at all points, they will lose interest. The false end is that moment where all your expectations appear wrong, when everything appears to be over but it isn't quite. When the psychopath appears to have been killed but suddenly turns up at a family party – when everything seems lost for the Alliance, until Darth Vader changes allegiances – when, in a documentary property programme, the buyer appears to be on the brink of pulling out. It's that moment, and it makes the final ending that much sweeter – or sourer – when it happens.

*Climax* – The moment when everything comes together – the final confrontation. In factual programmes, it's when the question posed at the beginning finally gets answered, or at least when the two sides of the argument are brought together most sharply. The climax leads to the resolution of the main dilemma and, if you're clever, it also brings all of the sub-plots to a neat close. This is the reason that so many films end in a big explosion: action, emotional content, sub-plots and the resolution of the main protagonists are all brought together in a single second.

*The Get-out* – You may need some summing-up at the end of your show to tie up the loose ends and give a sense of the way the story has changed your main characters or the way it's altered the viewer's perspective. However, make this as quick as possible – when the climax is over, the story is over, and you need to roll the credits as quickly as possible. After Frodo has thrown the ring into the volcano, finish the film – don't show scene after scene of his happy hobbit family for the next half hour. It just doesn't work.

It's also worth remembering not only that your overall program needs a story structure, but also that your individual scenes need to be treated in the same way. Each scene needs to feel a little like a story in its own right with the end of one leading to the beginning of another. Obviously, you don't want to apply all the storytelling rules to every shot in your programme, but every scene tells its own story. Even a series of shots showing someone making a cup of tea has a plot and an atmosphere and says something about all the characters in the scene. Even if your main character isn't making the tea, the way they're watching or ignoring, helping or hindering the tea-making process tells a story.

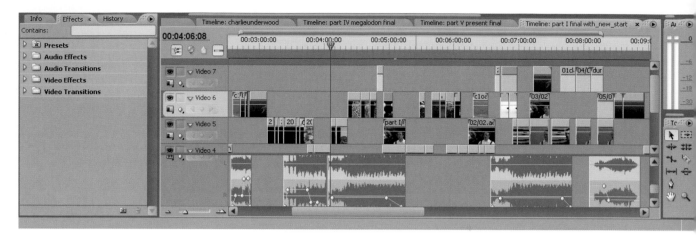

Fig 2 – A timeline shows every shot in your edit and can become very complicated, with layers of sound and picture.

Fig 3 – You can now output your video work in formats aimed at everything from the cinema screen to your mobile phone.

## THE EDITING PROCESS

Editing basically involves three stages:

1. *Getting your raw footage onto your computer's hard drive:* Video capture and assembling the various titles, effects, stills and music you're going to be using in the finished film.

2. *Cutting the footage together into scenes:* This is usually done on a timeline – a horizontal strip showing each clip as a box that can be stretched (to lengthen or shorten a shot), sliced (to cut shots in two) or moved around (to change the order of shots in your scene). Audio is also shown on the timeline and can be edited, layered and trimmed in the same way. As you build up your edit, the timeline can become very complicated with dozens or even hundreds of clips making up a programme, but the process remains the same.

3. *Rendering:* Once the edit is finished, you need to produce a finished version. This can be a file on your hard drive, a DVD, a tape, a file for the internet, or a mobile phone or iPod video. Either way, the computer will have to render out every frame of your video and every effect in the resolution and format of your chosen output medium. This can take hours, but the result is a finished playable video.

This three-stage method of editing means that you can work in any way you like. If you want to start at the end and work backwards you can. If you want to rough out your entire project and then move in to tighten up the details of each cut, that's fine too. If you want to work on particularly significant scenes or shots first and then assemble the rest of the production around them, or leave out difficult moments until you have the structure sorted out, that's no problem.

It's even possible to do a rough edit of your production before key shots have been filmed, by inserting proxy-shots or text screens to show what's supposed to be happening. That way you know exactly what you need to shoot when you come to filming.

The important thing to remember is that in computer editing nothing is forever. Nothing you do on the timeline affects your shots on disk. Any effects you add can be removed, and if you cut a shot too short, it doesn't matter because you can always drag it out to lengthen it again later.

## Types of cut

In editing, there are many ways to get from one shot to another. Editing has its own language and its own set of rules. It's worth at least being aware of several different types of cut:

*Straight cut:* The simplest form of edit. The picture and sound cut from one shot to the next. This is the most common edit in TV, film and on the internet. In fact to do anything else, you really have to have a good reason.

Generally you want cuts to happen so that the viewer isn't aware of them and simply feels they're naturally looking at whatever is most important. If you cut unexpectedly, or between two very similar shots (i.e. cutting out a section of an interview in which the camera doesn't move) you'll get a jump-cut. This is (usually) undesirable, and often needs to be covered with a cut-away.

*Dissolve, mix or fade:* Here, one image fades out and another gradually fades in. This can be done quickly (over a fraction of a second) to avoid jump-cuts or slowly (over a second or more) to show a gradual change, indicate time passing, or simply to create a more gentle transition between shots.

*Fade to/from black or fade to/from white:* These indicate an ending or a beginning. Audio and video fade in or out giving the impression that you're making a very definite break with what's gone before. Such a fade indicates that a chapter has ended or begun and gives the viewer a pause (of a couple of seconds) to digest what's happened and prepare themselves for what is to come.

*Wipe:* The image is gradually replaced by the next shot over time. Wipes are generally straight lines sliding from one side of the screen to the other, up and down, or diagonally, but there are many variations. Clock wipes replace the image radially like the hands of a clock. Other wipes can be in a variety of shapes from splattering paint to expanding love-hearts. Every video package contains a wide range of wipes, but they're used rarely as they can look slightly cartoony – "Meanwhile, at the secret hideout..."

*Figs 4–6 – A mix or dissolve can make the transition between shots a gentle one as well as communicating the passage of time.*

*Figs 7–9 – There are a whole range of unusual transitions available – just be sure to use them with restraint.*

*Fly in/out:* A shot flies off or onto the screen on a pre-defined course. A favourite of light-hearted entertainment and factual programmes, fly-ins are rarely used in fiction. They give an excitement to a shot, but are usually reserved for title graphics or for introducing segments of a show.

An awards ceremony might "fly in" a pre-recorded speech from a recipient unable to make it to the show. A magazine programme might use a fly-in or out to separate a location report from the studio section of the show.

*Transitions:* Broadly, a transition is any method of getting from one shot to the next, but it's often used to describe the huge array of special effects provided with most editing packages to manage scene transitions. These range from ripples to explosions to animations in which the shot folds into a paper dart and disappears off screen. If you really must use these effects, do so with caution, restraint and subtlety. Bear in mind most professional editors will never do anything more than a cut or a dissolve in any programme.

*L-cuts and J-cuts:* A sophisticated edit in which the sound cuts before or after the video (usually by a fraction of a second). This creates anticipation in the viewer. For example, the silence at the end of a poignant scene might be cut through by the sound of a phone ringing. A second later, we cut to the phone – beginning the next scene. This is a J-cut; an L-cut works the other way around: for example, an interviewee may be describing an event, and the picture cuts to that event for their last few words before the location audio begins.

*Cut-aways:* A cut in which the sound of the previous shot carries on throughout the new shot before the picture switches back to the previous image. This is a fairly common technique in all forms of programme-making.

An interview will often cut from the person talking to illustrate what they're talking about, with their voice continuing over the shot for a second or two. A drama scene will often include reaction shots or close-ups where the audio from the previous shot continues uninterrupted.

## Software

Editing software comes in a wide range of forms, but most of it follows a pretty standard layout and approach. There are usually four main windows in which your work is done:

*The monitor:* A TV screen showing your finished edit and offering VCR-style controls. The monitor might become jerky or blocky if you're adding lots of effects or picture in picture effects, but these problems won't appear in your finished (rendered) video.

*The bins:* A folder or set of folders containing all the video clips, stills, sounds, titles and often effects that can be used in your production. Anything that you want to use needs to be imported into a bin before it can be added to your timeline.

*Timeline:* A graphical representation of your entire edit. The timeline shows the edited show as a strip with tracks for audio and video, and each shot is illustrated as a block. Assembling an edit is just a matter of placing your shots at the right points on your timeline and cutting them to size.

*Controls:* Most editors offer some form of special effects. When you apply these, you need to be able to adjust their settings and controls. The controls window usually displays controls for whatever you have selected at the time. This can mean effects filters, transitions, DVD menus or video clips.

Depending on your editor, you may also discover other windows such as:

*Titler:* Allows you to add captions, titles and text screens to your movie, and may well allow you to alter text styles and colours, and add basic motions such as scrolls and crawls.

*Audio mixer:* Offers a selection of volume and stereo controls for each audio track as well as a master control for overall volume. The best mixers allow you to record your adjustments as the movie plays so you can (for example) adjust the volume of incidental music to fade in and out appropriately.

Fig 10 – A modern editing package may look complex but its windows are all fairly standard.

Fig 11 – An audio mixer is a common feature allowing you to control the volume of various tracks "live".

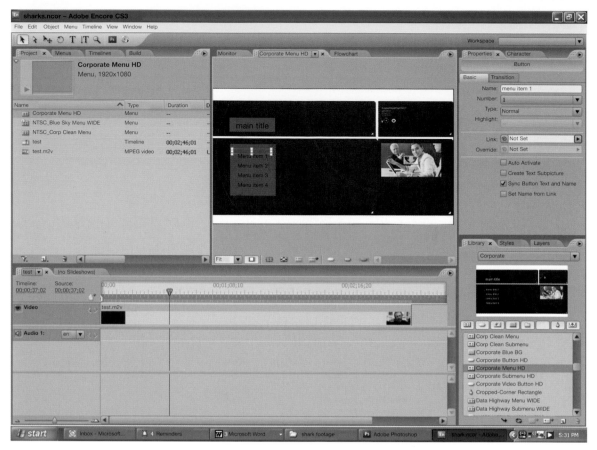

*Fig 12 – DVD authoring can be handled from your editor or from a stand-alone package.*

*DVD authoring:* This allows you both to create and edit menus for TV set-top-box disks. These usually make it fairly simple to create your own menus and combine several movies or clips on a single disk.

The cheaper packages (under £100) don't generally offer complex edits like L- and J-cuts and are often limited in terms of the controllability of their effects and transitions. You might also find they focus on one-button solutions for common problems such as exposure and colour correction and removal of camera-shake and audio noise.

Although these are useful, they're not professional tools and you'll usually find that the manual versions available in more advanced software are subtler and more open to fine-tuning.

### Capture
Your video material may have been recorded to tape, disk, DVD or memory cards, in which case it will need to be copied to your hard drive before you can edit it. If you're working with a laptop, you may have used a package like OnLocation to record directly to disk from your camcorder on set.

Either way, you'll end up with a selection of files on disk which will need to be imported into your editor's bins. Most editors offer the ability to automatically split up captured material into shots to make it easier to organize (although the software can make mistakes if your footage contains lots of movement or flashing lights).

### Editing – How to Make a Scene
As we've said before, editing is about telling a story. But how does this transfer to the process of putting one shot after another?

Well, to start with, it means that you have to have the viewer in mind at every moment of the process. You will need to tell them exactly and completely what you want them to know, while understanding precisely what they'll be thinking, what they'll be puzzled about and what they'll be emotionally involved in at every moment. Make no mistake – you are manipulating them.

Think of every scene as a story and tell that story with your cuts. Starting with a wide shot tells the audience where they are, who's in the scene and what their relationships to each other are. Cut to closer shots as the action begins and the audience will start to get involved with the characters. Move in very close when the audience needs to know details and they will be able to read every subtle nuance on the faces of the participants and see for themselves (for example) how close the safety rope is to snapping or how finely the garlic needs to be chopped in this particular recipe.

*Figs 13–14 – A classic editing sequence starts with a long shot to establish the scene, then moves in for more detail.*

*Fig 15 – When editing dialogue, pay as much attention to what's not being said as what is.*

The above is, of course, a very common pattern of editing – it crops up in every kind of programming from talk-shows to thrillers and is a good default for any scene. However, it's also important to use editing to hide information as well as show it – to create a sense of mystery and then slowly reveal the truth.

A horror movie or thriller, for example, will often contain a number of scenes where a character is shown in close-up most of the time. This use of close-up allows the audience to see the fear in the character's face, but just as importantly it hides everything else in the scene. What's behind the door? Where in the house is he? What was that noise? The fact that the audience does not know what's waiting in the shadows is what creates the tension.

Likewise, a documentary maker will often increase the drama by manipulating information for the viewer. The fishermen on a trawler may be fully aware as the storm picks up that it's a fairly minor one that offers little danger. However, that won't necessarily be revealed to the viewer as the waves crash on to the deck. The truth that working on a trawler exposes you to the danger of harsh weather is considered more important to tell than the truth that the only storm the documentary makers were able to capture was a mild one.

Probably the most important rule as you drag your clips to the timeline is to ask yourself two questions: "What does the audience want to know?" and "What do I want to show them?". Answer these two questions and you won't go far wrong.

## Editing Dialogue

Dialogue is not just a stream of words, and editing it is not just about cutting between one person speaking and the next. Two editors faced with the same sequence of dialogue will produce strikingly different scenes.

The reason for this is that what's being said with facial expressions, body language and other non-verbal communication, as well as what's not being said at all, is as important as the dialogue.

For example, if one character is giving information to another, it's generally the listener who needs to be in shot most of the time because the news is only as important as their emotional reaction to it. If two characters are having a conversation over dinner, it's not just the dialogue, but the way the characters eat, drink and gesture that can provide punctuation to the scene – a close-up of someone putting down a glass at a significant moment can be as powerful as a close-up on their face. Become an expert in body language because the dialogue is only telling half the story.

It's tempting to use close-ups all the time, but try saving them for the most important points in your dialogue – or the most important scenes in your story.

Also, consider inserting and removing pauses at significant moments by using reaction shots. You need to be aware of the rhythm of the scene as set up by the actors, but you don't need to slavishly follow it. Decide what's important, where the focus of the scene lies and how you're going to pace the scene.

If your scene involves several people, things become more difficult. The viewer has to understand everybody's place in it, and it becomes even more important for the editor to be clear about whom or what is the focus of the scene.

On a practical note, if there's a lot of movement within the scene, it somehow needs to be kept track of by the viewer. If a character suddenly pipes up from one side of the room when they started the scene at the other (or worse – not even shown on screen), then the viewer will be confused and disorientated.

## Editing Documentary

Documentaries are stories just like dramas, but they present their own editing difficulties.

Factual programming often contains a lot of interview material and you'll need to work hard to prevent a documentary from becoming simply

*Fig 16 – When editing documentaries you have to work hard to avoid too many "talking heads".*

a succession of talking heads. Liberal use of cut-aways allow you to edit down interviews to the salient points and help to illustrate those points more powerfully2. Constantly consider how you can *show* rather than *tell* your story.

Documentary edits often involve dealing with lots of raw footage. Interviews, particularly, are notoriously hard to edit (primarily because it's hard to find the ten-second quote you're looking for in an hour-long take). Consider getting a typed transcript made and using it to make a paper edit before you start. Also try doing a pre-edit in which you chop out only the clips you think you might use. This reduces the volume of footage you have to work with.

Narration can be useful, but bear in mind that every second of narration has to be covered with visual images. Most voice-overs will come in at around 120 words per minute, so keep to the point and be sure you have plenty of strong images.

## Editing Action

Cutting action is possibly the most challenging and rewarding job in editing. Action sequences often play fast and loose with the rules of normal sequences. There are as many ways to edit an action sequence as there are editors, but here are a few tips:

*Keep it short:* Most action scenes involve shots that get shorter and shorter as the action builds. Cuts every two seconds aren't uncommon and when in the thick of a fight, the viewer is barely given a few frames to register what's happening before it's over. This rule is often broken, however, and a complex stunt or choreographed scene is often shown without a cut, just to prove that it really has been done.

*Cut on action:* Cuts work best on movement and frame-accuracy is often essential. The moment of a significant punch in a fight scene can be a great time to cut to a close-up of the impact, but it you don't get it exactly right, it will look terrible.

*Long and short:* Try to cut from long shots to close-ups rather than stick with sequences containing similar framing. Remember, long shots tell the viewer what's happening, whereas close-ups involve them in it.

*Action and reaction:* Always remember that it's the emotional content of your scene that keeps people watching. Action isn't interesting on its own: what matters is your character's reaction to it. Make sure your audience is constantly kept up to date on where your characters are emotionally as well as physically. Without the reactions of the characters, the movie *Speed* is just a bus ride.

*Playing with time:* Time is relative. The editor can speed it up, slow it down, repeat it or even run it backwards and these are all legitimate tools of the action editor. Often, the most significant action shots in a sequence will be shown several times from different angles and a while a car chase across New York can see journey times reduced to few seconds, the crash that ends the scene can be stretched out of all proportion by slow motion.

*What the viewer knows:* You can create an action scene with virtually no action at all. The secret is to let the viewer know something that the characters don't know. Perhaps one of them is carrying a bomb. Perhaps a sniper has his sights on the building your actors are sitting in. Perhaps they're wandering happily around a house not knowing what lurks in the cellar. The tension that comes from the difference between what the audience knows and what the characters know can be one of the greatest tools the editor can call upon. The briefest action sequence at the end of the scene – or even none at all – will provide a pay-off for the tension you've created.

## Multi-camera editing

If your scene has been filmed with more than one camera, it can be a good idea to capture then sync up the shots on different tracks of the timeline with your master shot on top, and all but your best audio track removed. That way, you can cut the scene simply by chopping out chunks of the upper tracks, allowing the other shots to be seen.

Some editors allow you to work with multi-camera shoots in an even simpler way, playing through the camera shots at the same time and cutting from one camera to another as though the edit is being made live.

*Fig 17 – If you're shooting with more than one camera, you can often edit "as live", switching between cameras with a single click.*

Usually this involves numbering each camera and then simply hitting the appropriate number to cut from one shot to another. As long as the files from each camera have been synced up correctly and none are ever turned off during the shoot, you can edit your entire programme in the time it takes to play it.

The advantage of editing this way is that once the initial cut is done, your edits are placed on the timeline so you can fine-tune the edit and add dissolves and captions. It's the best of both worlds.

## Effects

But post-production doesn't mean basic editing. Increasingly it also means all manner of digital special effects. More than ever, advanced effects work is now within the realm of the desk-top videomaker.

An effects shot can often be the combination of several different special effects techniques. And so, rather than us telling you how to achieve certain effects, we'll take a look at the basic building blocks from which effects are built – either within your editing package or, in the case of more sophisticated effects, in a specialized compositing program such as After Effects.

The key here is that each effect can be "keyframed": in other words, many elements of the effect can be animated over a period of time.

*Image manipulation filters:* Just as there is a wide range of effects filters in still image packages including Photoshop or Paint Shop Pro, which make it possible for you to change the colour of an image, blur it, brighten it, distort it, etc. the same types of filters are available in editors and effects packages.

*Fig 18 – Image filters can have a dramatic effect. Here colour correction is used to change the uniform colours and make the background black and white.*

*Titling:* Another effect found on most productions. Titles can be as basic as a single page graphic or as complex as the most sophisticated animation. Basic rolls, crawls and fades are available in most editors, but if you want to animate each character individually or produce complex effects, you'll have to use a compositing package.

*Animation:* Taking any video clip or still image and animating its position, rotation or scale over time. Basic animation is often possible in an editor, but it really comes into its own when you start cutting out individual objects and animating them using other shots as backgrounds. Sophisticated packages will display a graph of the way an object moves and allow very fine control over it.

*Masking:* The absolute key to many effects is the ability to cut out any shape you can draw. Why? Because once you can mask an area of a shot, and

animate that mask (usually frame by frame by hand), you can remove single objects from scenes and place them into other scenes.

You can also apply animations to just one part of your shot or just one single object within it. Masking is usually done by drawing lines, then animating points on those lines. There's also usually a "feathering" tool to soften the edges of a line slightly so that objects from different shots can blend seamlessly. Masking is only available in specialist compositing programs and often means days of laborious frame-by-frame work.

*Keying:* Usually done by colour, keying is simply making an area of your shot transparent so that whatever image or shot you place underneath shows through. Most of the time, this means shooting action against a blue or green backdrop, then "keying out" the background to replace it with another shot. Many editors have basic keying tools, but they're not

*Fig 19 – Most specialist effects packages allow you to create graphs of the way each object in your scene moves.*

as good as the ones found in compositors. Keying always depends on how evenly lit the background is and how well defined the objects in front of it are and there's always a compromise to be made between the background becoming visible and parts of the foreground objects becoming transparent. If you're going to try this, make sure you don't move the camera, because, if you do, you'll have to make sure your background shot contains *exactly* the same camera motion – otherwise your background and foreground will appear to separate.

*Motion tracking:* Only available in specialist effects programs, motion tracking allows you to trace the movement of any object within the video frame. Why? So that you can apply that motion to another effects layer. This might mean superimposing a digital sign onto a moving lorry, adding a keyed (see above) object to a moving camera background or placing a 3D model into a hand-held video shot. Motion tracking (unless

you shell out thousands for the software) works in 2D, so it can handle up, down, left and right motion, but not zooming or moving around objects.

*3D:* OK, we're not going to tell you how to produce photorealistic 3D animation here. That's another book – or even a couple of them. However, if you've got 3D work already, you'll want to introduce it into your video edit as painlessly as possible. 3D animation can come to you in many forms. It can be produced as a standard video clip in the same format as your other footage. More often it will be a series of numbered stills, which are great if you want to work on them frame by frame in your still image editor, but not so good for playing back from the timeline (you may need to render them as video files before you can edit them smoothly). If your 3D work is a complete video clip then that's likely to be all you need to do. However, often you'll also need to composite the effects into video clips.

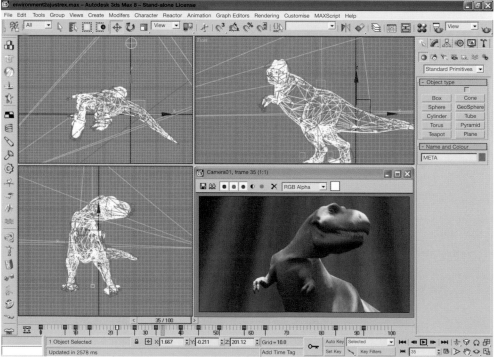

*Fig 20 – Keying is used to replace a single colour (in this case a green backcloth) with another image or video clip.*

*Fig 21 – 3D animation is a powerful tool, but it takes a while to learn.*

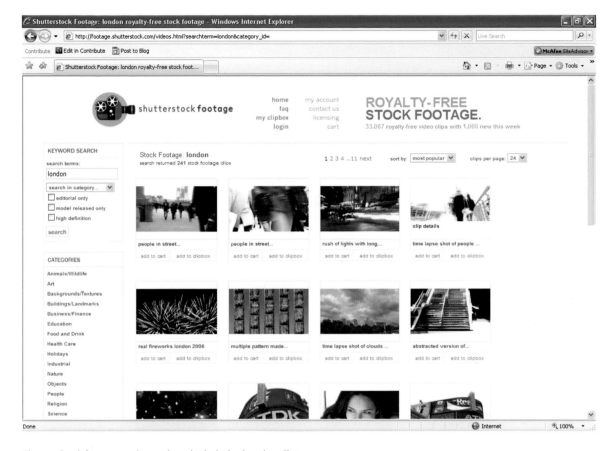

*Fig 22 – Stock footage can be purchased relatively cheaply online.*

As we've mentioned, these effects techniques are rarely used alone. For example, combine a mask with an image filter and you can make one object in a scene change colour. Apply keying to a title, and you can have a video clip cut into the shape of your words. Apply several layers of still images with animation and you can turn a graphic of a single spaceship into a whole fleet...

## Stock

You don't have to shoot your video in New York in order to set it there. Simply buying in a ten-second shot of the Big Apple, and cutting it in to the opening of your scene allows you to shoot it anywhere you like and people will assume that is taking place in New York.

This needn't be expensive. A large and expanding number of online libraries allow you to buy (and if you have a mind to, sell) royalty-free stock footage clips for a few pounds a throw.

Sites like iStockvideo.com and Shutterstock.com provide a trading place for videomakers and not only can you watch clips before you buy them and download them instantly, you can also search a vast library of shots at multimedia, DV- and HD-quality and be sure that whatever you purchase has all the appropriate rights secured for duplication and transmission.

Likewise, you can also use sites like Productiontrax.com to download royalty-free music in a huge range of styles. This is a great solution for incidental music, title themes and other background and foreground sounds. Prices vary, but £25–50 for a couple of minutes of professionally produced and recorded music is about average.

## Audio

Audio is imported, added and layered on the timeline in just the same way as video. Depending on your project, you may want to edit to the audio rather than the video.

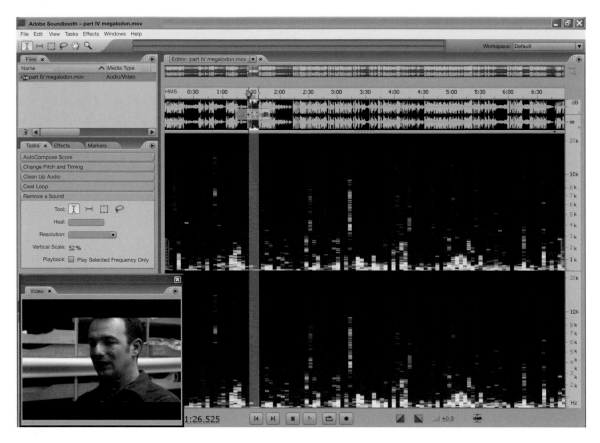

*Fig 23 – Advanced audio software displays your audio graphically so you can see unwanted sound.*

Pop videos will always be cut starting with the music and then synchronizing the video. Also, interviews will usually be cut first, based on what's said, and then later fine-tuned to make the visuals work. Dramas with incidental music tend to have the music written to fit the edits after a rough-cut has been created but, if you're using stock music, things can work the other way around.

Pay attention to the soundtrack and beware of pops and jumps caused by cutting from one shot to another. If you can, smooth things over with "wildtracks" – recordings of ambient sound made during filming which can be used to replace unwanted noises. Beware of "dead air" or holes in the audio. There's no such thing as complete silence – even the quietest room has its own background acoustic and it will become very obvious if there are gaps in your show's audio.

You can add spot sound effects, music, narration and background sound simply by dragging them to the timeline. However, sound editing can become very complex and timelines can become messy, so it's often helpful to designate different tracks for effects, background, music narration and so on.

Many editors include mixers – allowing you to control the volume and stereo positioning of each track with its own slider, so you can, for example, set the volume for the music throughout your programme in one go. Sophisticated mixers also allow you to play through a production, fading tracks in and out in real time, and recording volume changes live.

Audio quality is often a problem, and many editors offer filters and tools which can help improve the quality of your audio. These vary from simple graphic equalizers, which let you reduce the volume of (for example) very low sounds such as wind noise, right up to sophisticated tools that analyze your audio, and automatically detect and remove background sound.

There are also specialist audio tools such as Adobe SoundBooth, which offer incredibly sophisticated audio editing and clean-up tools: these include the viewing of your sound waves as coloured graphs on which unwanted noise can be spotted and cut out, in the same way you'd cut out an unwanted object from a photograph.

Be aware, however, that there are no magic solutions. Anything you do to remove background noise will affect and distort the rest of the sound, and voices may start to sound as though they're underwater or heard over the telephone.

## Export

Your finished movie will eventually have to be exported to be shown and most editing packages offer a range of ways to do this depending on the destination of your work.

A good rule of thumb is to export a full quality "master" of your project first. This may take a long time to render, but keeping a high quality copy and generating your other versions (i.e. DVDs, iPod videos, YouTube productions, etc.) from that will make your post-production easier in the long run.

If you're creating a disk (a DVD or high definition disk), you can choose to produce a simple disk which just plays your movie as soon as you put it in the machine, or you may want to "author" a disk with menus and a navigation system. Most video editors include a simple set of tools for producing DVD menus either from pre-designed templates or from scratch, and the process is simple enough to learn. This allows you to put several productions or versions of a production on to one disk, add alternative soundtracks and subtitles or include chapter points, so that viewers can jump to certain scenes or sections.

The one thing to bear in mind here is that the more you put on your disk, the more it has to be compressed, and so the lower the quality of your video picture.

*Fig 24 – DVDs can be created with or without menus.*

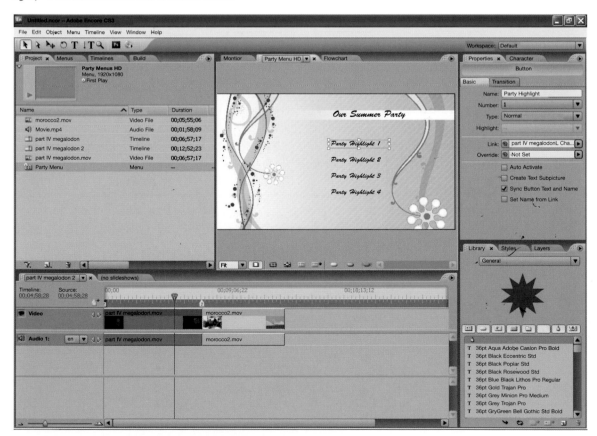

....DISTRI

15 – 24 november 2001
hotline 0121 212 0999
www.film-tv-festival.org.uk

17
birmingham film
and tv festival

# DISTRIBUTION

# DISTRIBUTION

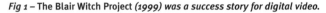

There's no point in making a video production if nobody ever gets to see it. Whatever your work, you'll eventually hope to find an audience for it. If your audience is just family and friends, then your life is easy. Invite them round and stick the DVD in the player, or email your work to them in a well compressed file.

If your audience is wider, you need to work harder. Thankfully, these days your choices for the distribution of your video productions are wider than ever. The internet is a massive and freely available broadcast medium which is open to anyone with the basic technical skills needed to put their work online. Film festivals are run all over the globe and many filmmakers with critically successful work find themselves on round the world trips even before their films are ever sold. Film and TV distribution deals are rare and complicated, but if your work is strong, well promoted and lands on the right desk at the right time, there's always the possibility of it being picked up by one of the burgeoning numbers of TV channels and film companies around the world.

## FILM AND VIDEO

It used to be the case that productions (particularly fictional films) shot on video weren't taken seriously. The medium wasn't considered high enough quality and there were all kinds of arguments about the texture and image quality of footage recorded on

*Fig 1 – The Blair Witch Project (1999) was a success story for digital video.*

*Fig 2 – Viewing your movie should be an event no matter what the location!*

film. Film was considered more atmospheric, softer and more dramatic. In addition most cinemas simply weren't set up to show digital material.

This lead to a sizeable number of filmmakers shelling out thousands of pounds to have their works transferred from video to film for showing at festivals, and many festivals rejecting the work of very talented filmmakers simply because their medium was video.

Today, many films – even top Hollywood movies – are shot on video. Many are still shot on film because of the differences in image quality and resolution. Some are even shot on video then processed to look like film. Hollywood rarely uses domestic camcorders – even HD ones – but well lit, well shot footage made on a decent enthusiast's camera is good enough for most cinemas, broadcast and all film festivals.

## GETTING YOUR WORK SCREENED

Shyness is a trait videomakers should banish from their personality. If you have made a video, you should want people to watch it and comment on it! It is very easy to sit in the comfort of your living room, and show your video to a select group of friends who will say "that's very good" or "that's nice". What you want is input from experienced videomakers who can tell you what worked in your video and what did not, plus, more importantly, why it did not work and how you can put it right. Always remember that digital video is a visual art and it therefore involves an audience being able to see it, and naturally, wanting to comment on it. There is a dazzling array of videomaking festivals that you can submit your work to – and we have provided a list at the back of the book – but not everyone wants to start that

*Figs 3–4 – The adrenalin rush from seeing your work screened makes the effort worthwhile.*

way, preferring to build up their videomaking skills slowly before putting them under the microscope of competition.

## GETTING TOGETHER

Often, the best first step in getting your work to a wider audience is getting together with some fellow filmmakers and getting comments from them. Even before the first tape has been shot, it can be a useful and instructive experience to get to know a few people who have made videos before or are in the process of making them.

There are video clubs around, and it may well be worth finding out whether any local ones are active and whether they cater for the kind of productions you have planned. Another source of potential collaborators is the internet. There are a range of email groups and web communities online who specialise in all kinds of video production –

Shooting People, Cinemaweb and DocoNet (for documentary filmmakers) are a few of the larger ones. On them you'll find discussions of all kinds of filmmaking techniques and dilemmas. It's well worth getting involved to learn from others and share your own knowledge.

Back in the real world, there are also a wide range of formal and informal film nights screening short films, and even works-in-progress. These have varying structures, requirements and audiences. Some will allow you to show a few minutes of your work and then open up the floor to discussion of it. Some will show a range of material over the course of an evening. Most take place in local halls or pubs and you can often expect to find other filmmakers as well as interested viewers so you'll get varied feedback for your work. Many filmmakers go along to a screening with a group of people involved in the production – this gives everyone a

chance to see the work on a big screen, but also provides a bit of support in what can be a nerve-wracking experience.

It's well worth checking out whether there are any in your area – not just from the point of view of showing your films but also to allow you to see how other people are approaching the problems you're facing.

## FESTIVALS

The short film is increasingly seen as a valid form of expression and audiences often realize that as much work has gone into a short film as a full-on feature. This is especially true, given the number of crew involved!

The UK has a very active festival circuit, catering for live action, documentary, animation and avant garde videos. Whatever form of digital video you create, there will be a festival out there for you to subscribe to. Naturally the selection process for

these festivals is stricter than for local film nights, and they can often have competition sections where you might end up actually competing alongside entries not just from Britain, but from Europe and also from the rest of the world.

There are also an incredible number of short film and video festivals the world over, and they usually take submissions (provided your video meets the theme) from whomever wants to submit their work.

The film department of the British Council publishes www.britfilms.com – a great website for filmmakers which includes a pretty comprehensive listing of national and international film festivals. It's well worth a look if you're contemplating the festival circuit.

Oh, and don't expect to get into Cannes with your first project.

### Meet the Criteria

Every festival has different procedures for accepting

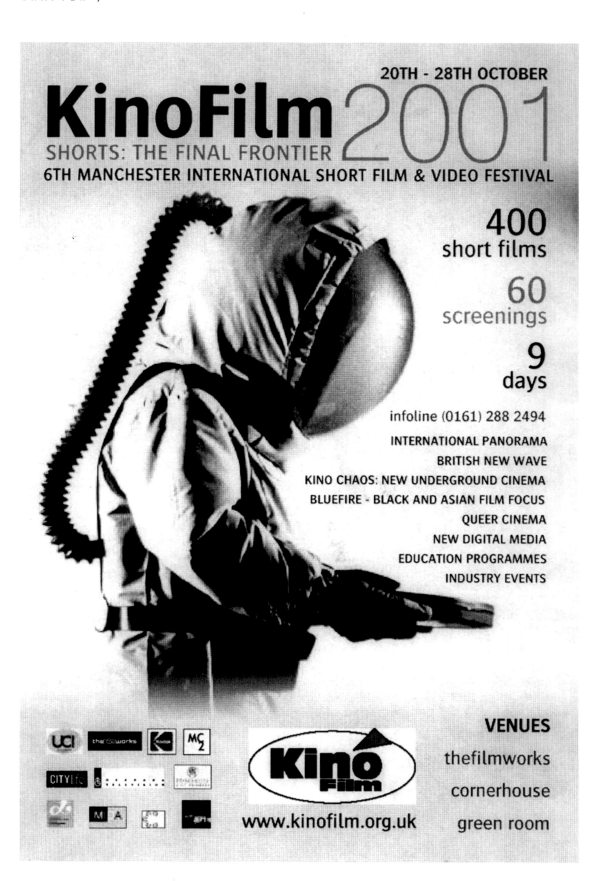

*Figs 5–6 – Most countries have a thriving short film and video festival circuit.*

entries. Read their entrance criteria carefully – there are usually so many entries for these festivals that you do not want to give anyone an excuse to file yours in the bin! Check in which format the festival wants to receive its videos and remember that what the organizers need to see is a whole package. You might think your video is absolutely fantastic, but you want to make sure the judges feel the same way. To do this they have to see the video, and if it is in a blank case with no details or publicity blurb then they might not get that enthusiastic. You have probably spent an immense amount of time and effort on making your video; do not fall short by not promoting it properly. Make sure your video catches their eye. Try and fashion a cover for it and if possible include information about the story/ subject, cast and crew on there as well. It is fairly straightforward to create titles for your video and

if you have a printer with your computer then you could even print out a still from your video as a cover image.

### Press the Flesh

If you do get in, and can get there, try and go to the festival yourself. Most of the bigger events have opening and closing shows, as well as talks, seminars and workshops during the event. This is useful, as it allows you to meet the organizers, along with fellow videomakers.

If you are seen around you can promote your video, and as a result you get a bigger audience for your screening, having made this breakthrough and being seen as an interested videomaker there is no end to the contacts you can make.

Even if you do not have a video entered into a festival, they are great events to attend. You get the

Figs 7–8 – The internet offers an invaluable way of getting your videos distributed and seen.

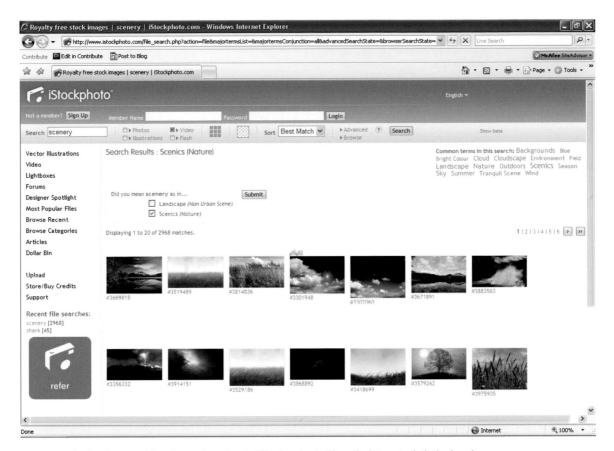

*Fig 9 – Royalty-free images, video clips and music can all be downloaded from the internet relatively cheaply.*

chance to see what your competitors are up to, and to check out the latest, cutting-edge techniques. As has already been mentioned, there are also workshops and seminars at many festivals. Even if you cannot get enrolled during the festival, the organizers often have training courses running all year round that keen filmmakers can join. Raindance, perhaps the UK's biggest independent film and video festival, is a good case in point. It runs courses all year round covering the basics and the advanced techniques of film and video production, from scriptwriting and storyboarding, to the different DV formats, lighting and editing. You may even run into a few of the people you've met online during the making of your work.

It is also worth keeping an eye out for what camcorder manufacturers are up to. JVC sponsors its own videomaking competition in Japan (Tokyo Video Festival), but entrants come from all over the world. Amateurs from the UK have a strong record in the event, and though the general quality is very high, you are not always competing with videos that cost thousands of pounds.

Sony has been keen to promote the work of young videomakers, and in the past has run day-long seminars with pop promo directors and videomakers who use digital technology in their TV shows.

## COPYRIGHT

Although it constitutes a book in its own right – a legal one – all videomakers keen to broadcast their own work should be aware of the issue of copyright. In the confines of your living room, you are usually safe to replay video and audio work without any fear of prosecution, but once you start looking towards an audience, there are rules you must be prepared to observe. These include using images from other films (such as a clip or still from a famous movie) and using copyrighted music (such as that from professionally produced CDs or DVDs).

Copyright can be a bit of a minefield, but here are a few of the basics. Any UK venue which exhibits your video – whether it is a community centre, village hall, exhibition centre, cinema or arena (ho ho!) – should already have a connection to, or licence with, the Performing Rights Society (PRS).

This means the venue pays a fee for the right to play music, whether that be the radio or a CD, and the PRS then sees that its members (songwriters, performers, producers, etc) get a percentage for the broadcast of the piece. You do not need to concern yourself with this, unless the venue does not have PRS connections. It will then be up to you to contact the PRS (address at the back of the book) and cement a deal with them.

**The Cost of Copyright**

What should concern you is that virtually all film and video festivals require you to clear copyright on your entries. This can simply mean writing to the copyright holder: film company, estate, music or publishing company and asking for permission to use the music, photo or video clip in your production. They can simply write back – and say yes or no! If they say yes, then there are a further two options. If the use of the copyright material is fleeting or negligible, then organizations will say yes, and usually not charge a fee. However, they can say yes and then charge a fee, in order for you to get clearance. Film and TV companies invariably have a member of staff whose sole job it is to gain copyright clearance for music and film clips. Fees are usually very high in this area, as the audience can run to millions, and a few seconds of a familiar tune (even if it is in the background) can cost a production company thousands of pounds. Companies and the estates who look after writers' and performers' rights, tend to be less harsh with amateur videomakers, though it is worth noting that the higher up the production scale your video goes, the more you will end up being charged!

The best thing you can do – and it's not expensive – is to buy your music from a royalty-free website. It will usually cost just a few tens of pounds or dollars (depending on the composer and performers) and you'll have unlimited rights to use the music within your production. You can also buy stock footage and still images in the same way. Again, prices vary depending on the resolution of the images and the rarity of the clip, but there are plenty of footage sites out there from which you can download a 30 second DV resolution clip for £25 (US$50).

It's not only music and video you need to secure the rights for, however. If you film on private property, or include trademarks, TV sets, recognisable brands or advertising banners in your shots (even in the background) you will be expected to be able to produce signed release forms. In addition, every person (even yourself) who appears in your work will have to have signed an agreement allowing you to use footage showing them.

As regards your own work, you need to know that there is no copyright on ideas, so you can only howl with frustration if someone comes up with a similar video to yours. That is unless you can prove that they have stolen the idea from you in the first place! However, the good news is that you own the copyright of any original footage you shoot – unless

---

**Copyright – the Facts**

- You cannot copyright ideas.
- You own the copyright to the material you shoot, unless otherwise agreed.
- Any other material you use will be covered by copyright (music, CD covers, photos, paintings, statues, books – written material, book covers, advertisements and packaging).
- Film and video festivals invariably require copyright clearance.
- Videomaking organizations have arrangements in place to help with copyright issues.
- Consider copyright- or royalty-free music. You pay a small fee and are entitled to then use the music in your video. It is also possible to purchase copyright/royalty-free video which is useful for creating backgrounds and titles. A list of companies offering copyright – and royalty – free material is included at the back of this book.

*Fig 10 – Thanks to the internet, your video can reach a global audience.*

you specifically assign that to someone else. This can be the case if you are shooting a video for a client and they express a desire to hold the copyright, or they include it in the contract you sign.

In any case, we would advise you to contact a recognized videomaking organization – such as the Institute of Amateur Cinematographers (IAC) – which can help you resolve any copyright issues. These organizations have often arranged their own deals for members with the PRS, MCPS (Mechanical Copyright Protection Society), PPL (Phonographic Performance Limited) or BPI (British Phonographic Industry).

### OPENING NIGHT – ONLINE

Now that most people have access to broadband, the internet has well and truly established itself as a way to distribute video. To the point at which there's a big question over just how long traditional transmitted

TV can hold on. What people are increasingly asking is "what is the point of spending millions of pounds transmitting TV via aerial, satellite and cable when doing it from a website costs nothing, is of comparable image quality and can potentially have a global audience".

It'll be a while before Crystal Palace gets turned off and Rupert Murdoch's satellites fall into the sea, and it's likely that the big players in broadcast will become big players online, but the revolution is beginning.

### Hosting

You can choose to host your film on your own website. If you do, you've got total control and can decide just how it's shown. However, it's often easier simply to upload it to one of the already-established movie sites. It will still have to compete for viewers, but the site will already have a promotions strategy

*Fig 11 – Every genre of film is catered for online.*

and the audience will at least be there, ready to be attracted.

Where you choose to host your film will have a direct bearing on how it's seen and whom by. Film sites come and go, and the medium is constantly developing.

Some have festivals on a given subject, some have tough submission policies and others none at all. Very few successful sites pay for online films and you're not likely to make any money no matter how many people watch your show. There are constant attempts to create a commercial way of putting your film out online, but none of these has really taken off (at least in terms of getting much cash for the average filmmaker).

There are also a growing number of sites like YouTube and MySpace, which don't pretend to be film sites, but which nonetheless host vast numbers of short video clips. The great thing about these sites is that you can upload any movie you like (within the site's obscenity restrictions) no matter how narrow its potential audience, then simply watch as your viewing figures and comments about your work roll in.

## Online publicity

If you host your video on a site alongside lots of other movies, the audience is likely to choose what to watch based on some kind of search engine. Search engines basically bring up a list of possible films based on keywords typed in by your potential audience members, so inputting the right keywords for your movie is probably the most important publicity job you can do for your online movie. Think of words that say what the movie is about, the themes it deals with, the subjects it approaches as well as words relating to its style and its genre. It's even worth putting in the titles of other movies with similar styles or themes – as you're aiming at similar audiences.

Make sure your title is both memorable, and easy to find in a search. Go to Google or another search engine and type in "Taxi Driver" – you'll get upwards of 6,000,000 hits most of which will have nothing to do with the Martin Scorsese classic. Now type in "the Ipcress File" and every result which appears will be about the film.

Whatever site your film is on, link to it every chance you get. The more other websites which link to your movie the more people will watch it. Get it reviewed, mentioned and rated. Publicising your film online is as time-consuming, as important and as competitive as it is in the real world. Don't put the work in and you won't get the viewers.

Of course, the potential audience for your film may not be enough for you to overcome certain reservations you may have about putting your film online. But maybe your film is just right for the medium, and maybe the idea of having it watched by people from locations as diverse as Kinshasa and Caracas really floats your boat. In that case, what do you need to do?

Well, it is remarkably simple. Once again, the advantages of digital video make themselves known. The chances are that your editing system already has what it takes to create an online movie, all you have to decide is how you are going to put it to use.

## Digital Video Formats

If you're hosting on a video site, the site itself will tell you how it wants your video encoded and it will decide how it's going to play it out.

However, if you're doing it yourself, you've got a choice of formats:

- *QuickTime:* Designed by Apple for the Mac, but available on both Macs and PCs, QuickTime requires the installation of a free player before viewers can watch your movies.

- *Windows Media Player:* Designed for the PC, and could be described as the Windows version of QuickTime. It can be used to compress files at a wide range of qualities.

- *RealMedia:* This format requires a special player. RealMedia's main innovation was to allow the hosting of non-downloadable files. In other words,

*Figs 12–14 – Media players, such as QuickTime, tend to look similar, but have very different capabilities.*

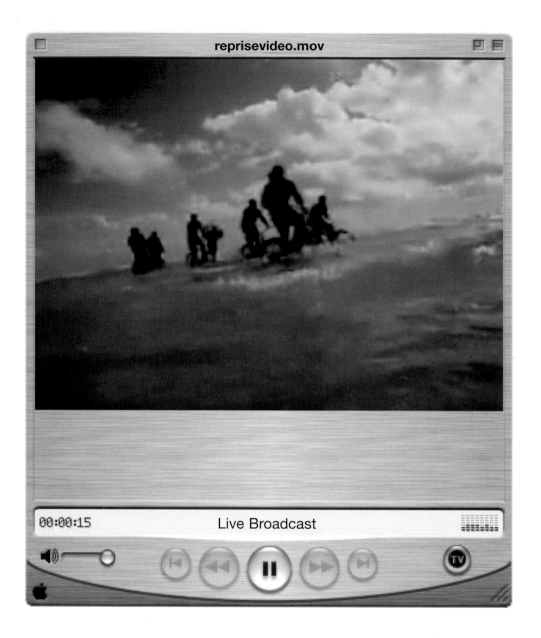

reprisevideo.mov

00:00:15    Live Broadcast

viewers have to come to your site to watch your movie – they can't copy it to their hard drive.

- *Flash Video:* This is the current flavour of the month. Flash Video is high quality, highly compressed and can be protected from downloading. It requires no special player, so works on 95% of machines, and it's part of Flash (the most popular tool in web design) so you can embed your movies in Flash websites and add interactivity to them.

*Fig 15 – RealPlayer is another of the most popular browsers.*

## Codecs

All these systems use **codecs** (COmpress/ DECompress) for compressing and decompressing video. Compression is the key to internet movies, and images on computer, in general. MPEG, which we have mentioned in several places throughout this book, is a form of compression, and the same goes for JPEG photographs.

Put simply, compression is a system of ignoring certain less important elements of an image in order to save space and then reconstituting that image based on the knowledge of what information has been left out. The codec is the method by which this compression is achieved, usually in the form of assumptions based on the changes between frames.

To explain this further, if frame one shows a blue vase and frame five shows a blue vase, and frames two three and four all show a blue vase, why not ask the computer just to remember that there are five identical frames rather than remembering five separate frames all showing the same thing.

Your editing package will have its own set of options for outputting movies and is very likely to be able to produce any of the popular formats. Presets are usually pre-programmed for encoding your video in a range of ways for a range of viewers. This will include not only internet video, but also the formats used by hand-held video players like the iPod and mobile phones. You can do all this by hand, setting any number of complex compression controls yourself, but we wouldn't recommend it.

Why do we recommend using the utilities to hand? Simply because you have already learned how to be a videomaker – believe us, you do not want the extra task of learning to be a webmaster, AV content producer and server technician as well.

It is this simple: try to do it on your own and you are in for a long, slow and disheartening learning curve. Use what is built into your existing software and you will be emailing the URL for your movie within a few hours.

:INTO TH

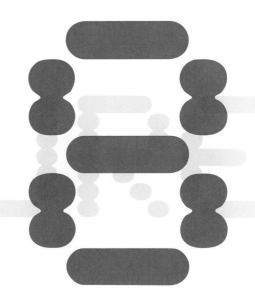

# INTO THE FUTURE

::::::INTO THE FUTURE::::

The world of video continues to expand and change. Everything, it seems is now a video camera, and everything is a video player. This means that video now comes in more shapes and sizes, resolutions and styles than ever before.

The videomaker (and that increasingly means everyone) now needs additional skills quite apart from the shooting, editing and storytelling skills we've discussed so far to produce compelling video content using these new and constantly changing media.

Here we present a few brief notes on how the newer media differ from those that came before, and what the prospective videographer needs to look out for in terms of style and technical challenges.

## VIDEOMAKING IN HIGH DEFINITION

HD means lots of detail. HDTVs might not be that much bigger than their predecessors, but they're much clearer, and this has implications for the videomaker.

First and foremost it means that every detail of your shot is there to see and needs to be right (and legal). If viewers can read the writing on a letter on the desk of an interviewee, you'll need to ensure it doesn't infringe anyone's privacy. If they can see an advertisement, logo or picture in the background,

*Fig 1 – High definition means extra detail, so pay attention to your background.*

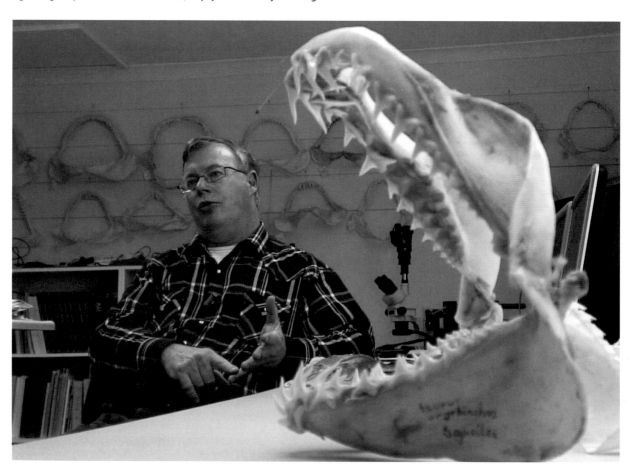

*Fig 2 – The screens of portable devices are small, but the sound quality is excellent.*

you need to make sure you don't need permission to show it.

The extra detail also means that you've got to work extra hard if you want to get away with hiding microphones in shot or gaffer-taping objects into place. Props in the background are more readily recognized, so you need to pay more attention to them, and poor finishing on your set will show up more clearly.

In addition, focus is far more critical in HD than in standard definition and given that viewfinders haven't increased in size, it's a good idea to have a decent sized monitor on location if you can. If you can't, just be very careful and use all the camera's tricks and features to get a good, sharp image.

## VIDEOMAKING FOR THE (VERY) SMALL SCREEN

From mobile phones to MP3 players, everything with a screen and a memory has become a video player. These new machines vary considerably and most have very small screens indeed. Despite this, people on long train journeys and in waiting rooms are increasingly using these personal video devices to view clips, video podcasts, music videos and even full-length films and TV programmes.

If you're making video podcasts, or any production with an eye to these new devices, the most important things to consider are the screens, and the distracted way the viewers will be watching them.

The screens are not, by and large, the same shape as TV or camcorder screens, and they're not a standard shape either. This means that you'll need to keep the important action as close to the centre as you can to ensure it's seen on every device. Forget artistic framing – the name of the game here is just getting the important stuff in shot.

In addition, we're not talking about High Definition – most of these tiny screens are just a couple of hundred pixels across. Detail just doesn't come through – everything needs to be big and bold. Text captions need to be minimal in terms of words, clear and large, and action needs to fill the camera's viewfinder.

Audio is far more important in ultra-small screen video than in any other type of programming. Viewers may not always be looking at the screen, but they'll always have the headphones in their ears, so crisp, detailed, intimate sound is possible and should be considered as your most powerful tool in getting through to your audience. Think of it as radio with pictures.

*Fig 3 – Video online has to be eye-catching and instantly engaging.*

## VIDEOMAKING FOR THE WEB

It used to be that compression was the biggest issue for video on the internet. With the rise of broadband, and the development of extremely powerful compression tools, you don't need to worry too much about pixilated images and stuttering motion. There's still a slight tendency for poorly compressed internet video to drop frames so that fast moving action sequences can lack fluidity and very brief shots can disappear. Also, video can pause when connections are not good, forcing the viewer to wait while the next few frames are downloaded. However, with a decent connection on the viewer's side and a reasonable set-up on the hosting website, you can offer up video playable on most computers anywhere in the world.

Nowadays, then, the biggest issue is not compression, but attention. The internet is a big place, and there's an almost infinite amount of content waiting to be seen. Buttons and links are everywhere, tempting viewers to move on to another video, another site. Distracting advertising flickers constantly so you're not just battling it out against a few TV channels. Your video is in constant competition against the whole sum of human experience which is there waiting just a click away.

Your clip doesn't just have to fight for viewers, it has to grab them and hold onto them for every second of its length. Web video is a game of instant gratification – give your audience five dull seconds in a row and they're off.

There's no point in starting your online film with a slow, gentle pan across a landscape – most viewers won't wait to see what's at the end of it unless they already know that your movie is going to give them something special. That's the harsh reality of internet moviemaking. You don't have to use the highest production values. You don't have to obey all the filmmaking rules, but you do have to be passionate, powerful and instant.

At least, that's the harsh reality on YouTube and MySpace and all the other unregulated sites where quality is completely random. If you want an audience who will stick around, you have to be a bit more selective about how you get them, and often you have to host your work on a site which has some kind of selection process – that way viewers will know that your work is worth watching before they click on it.

It's likely that, as computers replace TVs in the living room, such sites will grow to become the new broadcasters, and viewers will be willing to watch more in the way that they watch TV. However, as this

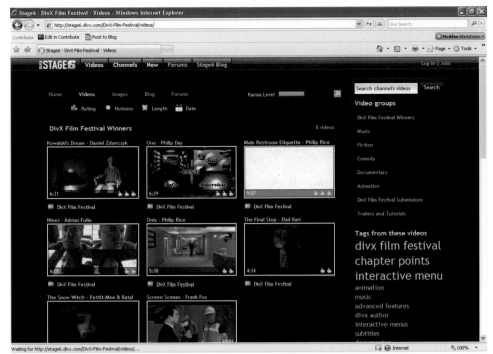

*Fig 4 – If you can get your film onto a site with some kind of selection process, viewers are much more likely to stick around.*

happens, viewers will also be able to choose their viewing from a menu consisting of everything that has ever been aired anywhere in the world, so competition will still be just as intense, if not more so.

## PORTABILITY

But video is video. It's unusual to shoot for one particular medium without there being any chance that your production will end up being transferred to others. What you most often want to do is record whatever you're filming in a way that can be as flexible as possible, and that means working to the highest quality you can and with the highest standards.

If you've got an interview shot on your mobile phone, emailing it to somebody else's mobile is pretty much all you can do with it. If you shoot on HD, line up a well balanced and composed shot, light it properly, ensure the focus is good and make sure the interviewee has a decent microphone, then the resulting footage will work well whatever format you eventually put it into. You can scale down, cut down and re-edit footage quite successfully for any format, but scaling it up, improving the quality or editing in footage that was never shot is much, much harder.

Do the highest quality work you can and you'll never regret it.

## FINAL THOUGHTS

There's a lot in this book. A lot of technical considerations and rules about how to compose a shot, how to write a story, and how to light, edit and format a video. However, all it really comes down to is the fact that video is a method of communication. It's a language. A language that everybody understands, but which most people are only just beginning to learn to speak. Once you understand how to communicate with video it's up to you to decide what you say and how you say it.

We hope that this book has given you some insight into the language of video and the confidence to pick up that camcorder and start using it effectively and creatively.

Because the real lesson of digital video is not about technical innovation – it's this: that the difference between the world's greatest filmmakers and everyone else is not so very much. With the advent of digital video, the technical differences are all but gone, the budgets are less important and the tools, both for making video and for delivering it to a global audience are increasingly available to all. The world seen through their viewfinder is the same as the world seen through yours, and the only requirement for creating compelling video is that you have something to say, and the determination to say it.

# GLOSSARY

## A

**Academy:** In this instance, the older format of film stock with an approximately square aspect ratio, later superseded by stocks with wider aspect ratios, such as 2.35:1 or 1.85:1.

**Algorithm:** A standardized set of rules or procedures for repeated calculations, in this case, for compressing and decompressing video with as little quality loss as possible.

**Anamorphic Lens:** A lens similar to a wide-angle lens except it only enhances the width and not the height, creating a widescreen aspect ratio.

**ARC:** Aspect Ratio Convert – the process of taking 4:3 footage and converting it to a wider 16:9 ratio (sort of a reverse pan-and-scan).

**Aspect Ratio:** The width-to-height ratio of the screen.

**Assemble Editing:** Editing whereby material is joined on the end of existing footage, without any changes at the edit point.

**Audio Dub:** The recording, or re-recording, of an audio track on a video, which leaves the existing audio untouched.

## B

**Backlight:** Light coming from behind the camcorder, which highlights the subject's outline.

**Blu-Ray:** A DVD format for high definition (HD) footage.

**Broadband:** Information delivery over a wide range of frequencies, allowing for a very high information capacity. In this case it is used to refer to a permanently connected high capacity internet service, as opposed to slower "Dial Up" services using ordinary domestic phonelines.

## C

**Capture Card:** A device that adds DV sockets to computers not already equipped with them, often subscribing to the OHCI (Open Host Controller Interface) standard.

**Cardoid Mic:** A partly directional microphone with a heart-shaped response field.

**Cast:** The actors in your film.

**CCD:** Charge Coupled Device – the image sensor that receives light from your camcorder lens and converts it into a video signal by assigning different values of electrical charge to represent the information contained by each pixel.

**Chrominance:** The video signal that defines colour.

**Codec:** A software or hardware item that applies algorithms to COmpress and DECompress your video signal.

**Compression:** The process of taking the huge amount of information contained in a video signal and compressing it to allow smaller and more easily transferred files.

**Continuity:** The method by which consistency and accuracy of costume, action, dialogue, etc., are maintained in film and video productions.

**Crash:** When your computer gives up the ghost in the middle of a task, displaying the notorious "Blue Screen Of Death" and resetting itself – usually sending your current projects to digital heaven in the process.

**Crew:** The people who carry out tasks behind the camera – camera operators, gaffers, grips, etc.

**Cut-away:** A shot used as a break or link between principal shots in a film or video.

## D

**Depth of Field:** The range of object distances from a camera, within which objects will be reproduced with sharpness and clarity.

**Dissolve:** The transition between two scenes where the first gradually disappears to be replaced by the latter.

**Download:** The act of importing a file from a remote computer to your own.

**DVD**: Digital Versatile Disc (sometimes referred to as Digital Video Disc) – a disc similar to a CD that stores video information in MPEG2 format. Capable of higher quality then VHS video tapes.

# E

**Exposure:** Exposure of the CCD to the correct amount of light, which is controlled by the aperture and shutter speed.

# F

**Filter**: A glass, gel or plastic disc which fits over the lens to create special optical effects.

**Firewire**: Aka IEEE-1394 or i.LINK – a high-capacity method of transferring digital video to other devices, such as a computer, and allowing those other devices to control the playback device.

**Framing:** The act of composing your shot and placing the elements of your composition in their required positions within the "frame" of viewable screen area.

**Freeze:** When your computer locks and refuses to respond to inputs from the mouse, keyboard or other devices.

# G

**Gaffer Tape:** Vital stuff – used to hold cables to the floor, repair broken objects, mark actors' positions on the floor, etc.

# H

**HDD or Hard Disk Drive:** The "long term memory" of your computer in which software and projects are stored. HDD camcorders record footage straight to their own internal hard drive.

**Hardware:** The actual "physical" components of your computer-processor, monitor, etc.

**HD or High Definition:** Video shot in HD is quite simply more detailed than DV footage. There are several formats, which are usually labelled 1080 or 720, depending on their vertical resolution.

**Hunting:** A slow response from the camcorder's auto focus system as it takes time to bring a frame into focus.

# I

**IEEE-1394:** Aka i.Link or Firewire – a data transfer protocol for moving audio and video footage, which also offers device control over VCRs and camcorders.

# J

**JPEG:** A photograph converted into a computer file according to the standards of the Joint Photographic Experts Group.

**Jump Cut:** An edit in which the perspective or framing or subject position between the two shots changes noticeably, causing items on screen to appear to jump out of position, creating a jump in continuity. Sometime used as a stylish dramatic device, more often just a stupid mistake.

# L

**Line, The:** In composition, an imaginary line drawn between parallel objects – if you begin shooting on one side of the line then move to the opposite side the two objects will appear to have swapped position.

**Luminance:** The video signal that defines brightness (measured in lumens).

# M

**Master Shot**: A complete shot of a scene made in a single take, in order to provide full coverage, usually used as a safety or back-up should anything go wrong with other shots. Master shots are not always practically obtainable, but if you can get one it's a good idea to.

**Media Player:** A program for playing back media files, such as video or music, on a computer. The major ones are QuickTime, Real Player and Windows Media Player.

**MPEG:** Motion (sometimes Moving) Picture Experts Group, a standard for compressing moving images into smaller files.

# N

**NLE:** Non-Linear Editor – a computer editing package.

# O

**Operating System**: The interface between yourself and various bits of computer hardware. Prominent operating systems include the various versions of Windows, Mac OS, Linux and Unix.

**OHCI:** Open Host Controller Interface – an agreement that allows various manufacturers to standardize their equipment for compatibility.

**Omnidirectional Mic:** A microphone that is equally sensitive in all directions.

## P

**Pan-and-Scan:** The process of transferring a wider cinema image to a narrower television screen by panning around the frame and scanning the important elements, while discarding the rest.

**Pixel:** Short for Picture Element, this is the smallest image part of a digital picture.

**Processor:** The brain of your computer that essentially reduces tasks and problems into millions of "yes", "no", "and" and "or" choices.

## R

**RAM:** Random Access Memory – the "short term memory" of your computer, which stores things that are currently in use and passes information to the processor.

## S

**Shooting Ratio:** The ratio between footage recorded and footage required. A shooting ratio of 3:1 would imply that three minutes of video are shot for every one minute that makes the screen. Used by Producers and Directors as a rough guide for planning how much tape is required; used by accountants to bemoan the amount of money spent.

**Shotgun Mic:** A highly directional microphone that can be aimed at its sound source.

**Slide Adaptor:** A device used for transferring still images from slides to video.

**Software:** The programs used on a computer.

**Stepping Ring:** A device with screw threads of different diameter on either side, used when the threads on the lens barrel don't match those on the device you intend to screw into the lens barrel.

**Streaming:** A method that allows a file to be played back as it downloads.

## T

**Telecine:** The process of transferring video to film stock, available in a variety of methods, of various qualities, at various prices.

**Timecode:** A coding system for audio and video for synchronization and editing. The timecode shows hours, minutes, seconds and frames – e.g. 01:12:58:02.

## U

**URL:** Universal Resource Locator, otherwise known as a web address.

**Unidirectional Mic:** A microphone that is sensitive in one direction only.

## V

**Vignetting:** The loss of picture area that happens when using an Anamorphic Lens at its widest setting.

**VCD:** DVD's little brother, which uses MPEG1 compression on a CD – similar in quality to VHS.

## W

**Wizard:** A software tool that takes you through a complicated process in a step-by-step fashion.

# USEFUL INFORMATION

## VIDEOMAKING ORGANIZATIONS

*Institute of Videography*
www.iov.co.uk
Central Office
PO Box 625
Loughton
Essex
IG10 3GZ
0845 7413626
020 8502 3817

*Institute of Amateur Cinematographers (IAC)*
www.theiac.org.uk
Global House
1 Ashley Avenue
Epsom
Surrey
KT18 5AD
01372 822 812

*New Producers' Alliance*
www.newproducer.co.uk
www.npa.org.uk
The Tea Building
56 Shoreditch High Street
London E1 6JJ
020 7613 0440

*The Guild of Professional Videographers*
www.gpv4u.co.uk 11 Telfer Road
Radford
Coventry
CV6 3DG
024 7627 2548
0845 165 1937

## USEFUL WEBSITES

### Online Films And Animation

www.atomfilms.com
www.thebitscreen.com
www.ifilm.com
www.newvenue.com
www.nextwavefilms.com/

### Magazines

www.computervideo.net
www.digitalvideomag.co.uk

### Information and Resources

www.bfi.org.uk
www.channel4.com/film/
www.cyberfilmschool.com
www.filmmaker.com
www.plugincinema.com
www.projector.demon.co.uk
www.raindance.co.uk
www.shootingpeople.org
www.simplydv.com
www.whorepresents.com
www.widescreen.org

### Scripts

www.howtowritescripts.com
www.scriptservices.com
www.shootingpeople.org
www.wordplayer.com

### Camcorder Companies

*Canon (UK)*
www.canon.co.uk
worldwide: www.canon.com

*Hitachi*
www.hitachitv.com

*JVC*
www.jvc.co.uk
worldwide: www.jvc.com

*Panasonic*
www.panasonic.co.uk
worldwide: www.panasonic.com

*Samsung*
www.samsungelectronics.co.uk
worldwide: www.samsung.com

*Sharp*
www.sharp.co.uk
worldwide: sharp-world.com

*Sony (UK)*
www.sony.co.uk
worldwide: www.sony.com

*Thomson*
www.thomson-europe.com

# INDEX

# PICTURE CREDITS
PICTURE CREDITS

**Original Illustrations by Geoff Fowler**

The publishers would like to thank the following sources for their kind permission to reproduce the pictures in this book:

**Adobe®** 117.

**Advertising Archive** 10, 47.

**Courtesy of Apple** 143, 144, 145.

**AtomShockwave** 138b, 142 © 2002 AtomShockwave Corp. and its licensors. All Rights Reserved. "AtomFilms" and the Logo are trademarks of AtomShockwave Corp. and may be registered in one or more countries. Other trademarks are owned by AtomShockwave or its licensors.

**Courtesy of Adrian Bentley** 37b, 58, 59, 96t, 105.

**Birmingham Film and TV Festival** 131.

**Brand X** 22t.

**Buzz Pictures** 40.

**Canon** 13.

**Canopus®** 23b.

**Carlton Picture Library** 44t, 68tl, 69, 76, 90.

**Cokin** 26b.

**Corbis** 43, Craig Aurness 67t, Bettmann 56, 60, 90t, Anna Clopet 106b, Pablo Corral 55, CRD Photo 99, Richard Cummins 59t, Dennis Degnan 120, Duomo 39, Paul Edmondson 51, Randy Faris 35, Mitchell Gerber 90, Kevin T.Gilbert 80t, Rod Goldman 41, Philip Gould 61b1, 61br, Mark Hanauer 57, Walter Hodges 48–49 & 54, Manuela Hofer 53, Jack Hollingsworth 133, Lyn Hughes 107b, Dewitt Jones 61t1, 61tr, Ed Kashi 32–33, Lawrence Manning 37t, Marc Muench 90br, Charles O'Rear 96b, Joaquin Palting 7 & 34, Caroline Penn 105, Picture Press 95, Paul Russell 98, Phil Schermeister 141, Paul A.Souders 100, Chase Swift 59b, Ron Watts 27t, 52, Roy Morsch/Zefa 3.

**Courtesy of Christin Darkin** 22b, 24, 38, 64, 65, 72, 82, 112, 114, 115, 118, 119. 121, 123, 124, 125, 126, 128, 129, 147, 148.

**Dell** 23.

**Edinburgh International Film Festival** 137.

**Electronics INC** 12.

**R. Follis Associates** 27b.

**Getty Images**/ Paul Avis 106t, 107, Cherie Steinberg Cote 84 & 85, Antony Edwards 81t, Ghislain & Marie David de Lossy 17, Patti McConville 81-second-from-top.

**Ronald Grant Archive** 66br, 66t, 78b, 83, 25t, 46t, 87.

**Hitachi Home Electronics Ltd** 19t , 21, 42.

**Courtesy of iStockphoto** 139.

**JVC UK Ltd** 14, 30b, 44b.

**Courtesy of Kobal Collection**/ DreamWorks/Universal 31, Twenty Century Fox 62, 63 b, 63t, Cruise/Wagner 66bl, Artisan Pictures 87, 88, 132, Warner Brothers 90bl, Universal 134.

**Manchester International Short Film and Video Festival** 136.

**The Moviestore Collection** 46, 50, 56.

**Courtesy of MySpaceTV** 150.

**Nokia** 15.

**Courtesy of Kevin Nixon** 11t1, 11tm, 11tr, 25, 26t, 28tl, 28b, 28tr, 29tl, 29tr, 30tr, 30tl, 67b, 70t, 70b, 73t, 82.

**Stephen O'Kelly** 68bl, 68b, 68tr, 73b.

**Panasonic Consumer Electronics UK Ltd** 18br, 19b, 20, 36.

**Popperfoto** 92.

**Rex Features Ltd/Timepix** 78t.

**Sharp Electronics Ltd** 45.

**Shutterstock Footage** 127.

**SONY** 11b, 18bl, 29b.

**Courtesy of Stage6** 151.

**Topham Picture Point** 81-third-from-top, 94 /Chapman 135, Photonews 81b.

**Vancover Film School** 74 & 75, 77, 80, 89.

**We're So Happy Films (Steve Thomas)** 93, 102, 103, 104.

**Courtesy of Vega Herrera Family** 16, 86, 101.

**Courtesy of YouTube** 138t.

Every effort has been made to acknowledge correctly and contact the source and/or copyright holder of each picture, and Carlton Books Limited apologises for any unintentional errors or omissions which will be corrected in future editions of this book.